A Hypnotist's Journey

to

The Secrets of The Sphinx

Sarah Breskman Cosme

D1716296

For permission, serialization, condensation, adaptions, or other publications, write to the author at https://www.theholistichypnotist.com

Other books by the author: A Hypnotherapist Journey to Atlantis. Also available in Spanish and Latvian.

A Hypnotist Journey to Atlantis provides information obtained through various subjects by hypnotic past-life regression.

1. Hypnosis 2. Reincarnation 3. Past-life regression 4. Metaphysics 5. Atlantis 6. The Sphinx I. Sarah Breskman Cosme

Cover Design: John Cornwell
Book set in: Garamond

ISBN: 979-8793266895

DEDICATION

Thank you to all my friends and family for your love and support.

Thank you, Dolores Cannon and Julia Cannon, for your help throughout this book.

Thank you, Jen and Christie, and all my clients for letting me share your stories that made this book possible.

Dear reader, this book is dedicated to you.

"The truth shows up as nothing more than a rumor at first, and behind the façade of the rumor are the triggers which eventually lead the mind to the acceptance of this truth. The sacred information within the Sphinx is no different. There are many who are not prepared to hear the truth, and so, for them they will see this as a rumor and that is ok. We will say that for some this will excite, for some this will give them deep peace, and for many, this will change their lives forever."

~The Higher Self

INTRODUCTION

The information within this book has been carefully gathered using Quantum Healing Hypnosis Technique, otherwise known (and referred to) as QHHT, created by the late Dolores Cannon. In a QHHT session the client is regressed, led only by their own intuitive higher guidance team, and brought to the deepest level of trance where their higher self is then accessed. Therefore, it's important to understand that I did not write this book. Every time I thought this book would go in a certain direction; the information would surprise me by going in a different direction altogether. I feel that is just the way with this information; I can't lead it, project its direction or plan for it. Instead, the information comes when the higher consciousness is ready to come forth with it.

I initially discovered this and documented it in my first book, "A Hypnotist's Journey to Atlantis." In this book I reported how through several QHHT sessions with a woman named Jen, I helped her recall numerous past lifetimes through which we uncovered, and then spread, vital information for the world to learn about the ancient civilizations that were once called Lemuria and Atlantis.

Once "A Hypnotist's Journey to Atlantis" was published, I was overwhelmed by an outpouring from readers who reported that they felt the information in this book served as a type of catalyst for their own healing journey. One reader commented that her son, who she had remembered in a past life as an animal child, who had been taken from her, had developed a strange cough in this life that went away as soon as this story was uncovered. Another reader proclaimed that their eyesight cleared up upon reading these words. It is my hope that you find peace and healing throughout this book as well. It is my intention to bring back what was once lost so that you may understand who you really are and what your true purpose is in this lifetime, and optimally, I hope this book serves as a catalyst for your own healing. This information is desperately needed now as we embark into new phases of our human development. I am just your humble messenger, relaying the words that have come through the higher selves of my clients.

Dear reader, this book is as much mine as it is yours. And by picking it up to begin with, I am certain this information is looking for you as well. This book is dedicated to you.

Table of Contents

CHAPTER 1: A WOMAN NAMED CHRISTIE

After publishing "A Hypnotist's Journey to Atlantis", I eagerly wanted to continue working with my subject Jen to uncover more information about the aftermath of the lost civilizations of Lemuria and Atlantis. However, as with any QHHT session, there is no telling where the higher self will take my client and where our journey will go, and with Jen it was the same. We had previously learned that sometime around the 1970's, Jen had uncovered and tried to share this forgotten information, only to be called crazy, lobotomized and eventually kill herself. Upon working together again, we quickly learned there was much more to this story that still needed to be uncovered, and for this reason the higher self took us there. Below is our session and the beginning, or you could say, the continuation of our story.

S: Let's drift and float to the most important time and place that has information that we would like to find, to help you, in the very best way that we can. What do you become aware of?

J: I seem to be in a high school and I'm walking down the hall. All the lockers look very narrow and painted with a bright orange, burgundy and yellow color, and these colors are made into a repeating pattern throughout this hallway. It has this weird effect when it ripples down the hallway with that pattern and color. Looks like the halls are very empty, everyone's in class. I can see the classrooms as I'm passing by the doors.

S: What does it look like inside the classroom that you pass by?

J: It looks like it's almost summertime and all the windows are open. There are these long vinyl sheets that cover the windows that you pull down that look like long canvas and plasticky looking things. The sun is beating in through the room and the kids look like they are all sweating because they're all wearing cotton, and most of them have their shirts open at the top to let in some air, because it's so hot.

S: What do the desks look like?

J: The desks are a combination of wood and metal. They are all one piece, and the chair connects to the front of the desk. The wooden part of the desks has a high gloss to it and the metal has like a greenish tinge to it.

S: Why are you in the hallway?

J: I don't feel well. I have a pass that I've gotten and I'm going to the nurse's office. I feel sick from the fight that I had this morning with my mother and her husband.

S: Tell me about this fight.

J: I woke up to the sound of him screaming, yelling at us both. He was yelling at my mother first, and then at me, for no reason. He was just in a bad mood because there was no milk left. He has coffee in the morning, and the milk bottle was empty and that made him just flip out completely. He pulled my mother out of bed by her hair and dragged her down the steps. Then he opened the fridge, which was a seventies looking fridge, and threw the milk bottle across the room at her. I could hear the loud crack as the glass shattered all over. I ran downstairs to see what was going on and when I got down there, he started yelling at me the second he saw me. He suddenly diverted his anger at me instead of her as she was heaped over crying on the floor, trying to pick the pieces of the milk bottle up, and cutting her hands. Her hands were full of blood dripping from her fingertips. I remember her two fingertips looked the worst. They were full of blood, the middle one and the pointer finger, and it was grotesquely mixing with the glass on the floor. There was a lot of blood. The blood was dripping out and the cuts looked very deep, and I thought to myself that she must need stiches. My mother's husband said that he wouldn't let me bring her to the hospital! Instead, he kicked me out of the house. He told me that I had to go to school and get out of this house.

S: Is that what you did? Did you go to school after that?

J: I did. I grabbed my stuff up and I got out of the house as quickly as I could. I hadn't showered or washed myself, but I had thrown on some clothes from the day before that were on the floor and grabbed my bag and I ran.

S: Why did you go to the nurse's office? Why did you feel sick?

J: I felt like I was going to throw up, I had so much anxiety flowing through my body. I felt so much anxiety that it was almost like an adrenaline rush, and I didn't know how to deal with it. I couldn't focus on school so I decided to see if the nurse would just let me lay down on the cot that they had set up in her office.

S: What does the nurse's office look like?

J: It's long and rectangular and a bit narrow, it looks like a railroad apartment where the front part is her desk and then behind her is a door and what looks like a long hallway. And off the hallway and to the left-hand side are four different small rooms that each have a cot and a single light set up in each of them. These rooms are usually empty; there are just a few of us who are in them at a time.

S: Is anyone else in there with you today?

J: No, there's no one there today. No one really wants to go to the nurse's office. They would rather just leave the school if they don't want to go to class.

S: And how would you describe your day-to-day life during this time?

J: Very stressful. I felt an extreme amount of anxiety. I woke up with it every morning and fell asleep with it, and I would even dream stressful dreams constantly. I felt as if I was just waiting for someone to start screaming in the middle of the night and this whole cycle of violence and abuse would start again with my mother's husband.

S: *During this time did you have any friends?*

J: I didn't because I wanted to keep to myself. I didn't want anyone to come over to my house, or to know how my family really was, and I avoided people, but they didn't understand why. They just thought that I was being very standoffish, and because of that many people would avoid me or just make up stories about me.

S: *Ok, let's leave that scene and move ahead in time in that same lifetime to where something important is happening. What do you become aware of?*

J: I had been feeling a lot of anxiety that day and had gone to sleep with it, and the anxiety even affected my dream where I was experiencing a nightmare, and suddenly, I wake up and I feel frozen and suspended. I can't move. I can't change my face to show emotion, every part of me is frozen.

S: *What do you mean by frozen?*

J: Not cold, but just unable to move or to express anything with my body. I can't move my arms or my legs, but it's more than that. I can't smile, close, or open my eyes. I can't do anything with my face. I want to scream, but I can't scream, I can't do anything! It feels like I'm in a coma even though I'm not.

S: *What were you doing when this happened?*

J: I was just sleeping in bed…I think something scared me…something in the room, it made me wake up. Whatever woke me up was over by the window and it felt like someone was looking at me and it scared me.

S: *Was someone looking at you, or no?*

J: Yes, someone was looking at me. One of these beings that you would label as extra-terrestrial was there. I can only see this now from an after perspective, because when it was happening to me, my mind didn't let me see this for my protection, and this was done in a way that wouldn't affect my psyche.

S: *What or who was it really?*

J: They were beings from my home planet, the Pleiades. They were able to levitate me out of my environment in order to check on me and see how I was.

S: *Why?*

J: Because they knew that I may need some adjustments, and they wished to do a checkup on me.

S: *So, you find yourself frozen after you are scared awake. What happens next?*

J: I feel the need to leave my room and go across the hall to my mother's room, but this light that comes down stops me. And suddenly, I'm lifted up. My arms are at my sides, and I can't do anything. It just holds me there, suspends me for what feels like a couple of moments and just holds me in place. And then this light just slowly starts bringing me down the stairs. I feel like I'm almost in an angled sitting position with my legs out in front of me and then a bit bent at the hip, and I'm taken down the stairs like this and then out through the front door.

S: *Are you awake when this is happening or is a part of you still asleep?*

J: No, I'm awake. I remember trying to look around me, but my eyes could only look forward. My eyes were frozen as well, and I couldn't even get the peripheral vision because this light freezes all of you. It just keeps me in suspended animation.

S: *Do you know why you are frozen like that?*

J: It's easier to transport me like this. They can't just walk into the house and throw me over their shoulder.

S: *And is a part of you still in bed? Or is all of you there suspended?*

J: All of me is being suspended and taken, all of me. It doesn't feel like I'm sleeping or that anyone has left me in bed and just a part of me is going to them. This feels very physical.

S: *What happens next?*

J: I am taken all the way down the stairs and then the front door opens on its own. And I am gliding out, and there are these lights that I can see coming from outside. They are blue, red, white, yellow and a bit of orange as well. It's like a light show. They are very bright, and the lights are shining from the bottom and around the sides of this large circular disk above me. This large circular disk is a light silver, titanium-looking color. It is an extra-terrestrial ship.

S: *Tell me more about that. What else do you notice about it?*

J: It's very big. It's so big that it could easily fit many of the houses we have on this street inside of it.

S: *What happens next?*

J: There is another light, a white light that shines down from the middle of the ship. This light mixes with the yellow light beam that I'm currently in and pulls me up all the way into the ship.

S: What happens next?

J: Everything went black all of a sudden. It feels like they put me to sleep because they see or understand that I'm still conscious and they knock me out somehow.

S: How do they do that?

J: It is a telepathic way of inducing sleep in humans that is similar to a kind of mind control that doesn't need any type of drug to knock someone out. It's just simply something that they can do with their minds to cause me to go to sleep.

S: Do you get a sense as to what it is that they do?

J: It feels like a kind of radiation that comes out from the center of their foreheads towards me and when it does it just makes everything go black. So, you're in that same suspended animation but now you don't have to think or see anything. And you're not aware of what's going on around you. You do feel like you are still awake on some level, but you also feel like you're stuck in this dark cylindrical tube, waiting. You can't understand or perceive or feel what's going on around you. You have no idea of what that is, but it's not a dream, there's no dreaming. There's nothing that you go to, and interact with, or escape to. It just feels like a very dark quiet place of waiting that is just meant to subdue you.

S: What is happening while you are knocked out like this?

J: The extra-terrestrials (ETs) are scanning me with these long rectangular devices that have a blue light that comes out from them. They are just looking to do a checkup, it's like going to the doctor almost. There's much love in what they are doing. It's not meant to be harmful, or in any way hurt me. It's actually very beneficial in many ways that they are doing this.

S: How does it benefit you?

J: They work to even things out in my body and my mind so that I can continue and persist with the mission that I have set forth in this lifetime.

S: Why would your body have issues?

J: The anxiety that I was experiencing was interfering with my ability to tap into what I was supposed to tap into. The anxiety was blocking it out. There was so much anxiety in my life that it was even affecting my stomach in a harmful way. It was affecting the way I was internalizing the world around me.

S: Did they fix this for you?

J: They fixed it so that it could maintain itself permanently in a homeostasis where I could continue and go on.

S: Can these ETs heal whatever it is you want them to heal?

J: Yes. As long as it's something that works with the contract that you've created. But if the issue is something that is part of your contract and something that you are looking to experience, then they are not allowed to interfere.

S: So, what did they heal exactly?

J: They are very responsible for me being able to overcome much of my anxiety and difficulties as a younger child in that life. It looks like they balanced a lot of things out within my body, there were things that would've been worse. Things would've been a lot worse if I didn't have this type of interaction.

S: So, on this day when they're scanning you, what do they do to you exactly?

J: They do many different scans, and they give me a type of healing energy that is meant to calm my anxiety so they can make sure that it doesn't internalize too deeply within my body. Sometimes, in previous contacts with them they would even remove me from abusive situations and instill me with the ability to go on and heal the wounds that were created. This would also allow me to go within myself to understand my situation better, and to persist, it seems like persisting is a big part of it. It almost feels like they are there at the end of the marathon to cheer you on giving you water and orange slices, like they are there to watch you succeed and to help you in any way they can. But you are the one doing the running. But they remind me of the plan I chose before I came into this life to see if the interaction with this abuse would actually help inspire the writing, creating, and bringing that message out to people. They realize now that we were all too eager, this was just not the right time.

S: Is there anything else about that that looks interesting or important?

J: There's a very strong connection between the lifetimes we live and those who are a part of this ET contact.

S: What do you mean?

J: It may look very generational for some people with some species of ETs who have come here. But for others it is a lifetime thing where they have followed your eternal being, your soul. They are monitoring your soul, that is what they track. And they know who you are because you are part of this larger system.

S: What are you part of exactly?

J: We are part of this big universal type of federation. It is very eternal, old, and very powerful. It is all knowing and feels like it has this godly presence to it, but it isn't one individual, and it isn't multiple gods or saints or anything that religions would have interpreted it as. But there seem to be many players in this federation. This federation could best be described as a group of eternal beings that take many forms and use many methods of interacting with each other.

S: Is that the group that you are in?

J: Yes, I feel that I am very deeply a part of it, and I feel that during my incarnations on this planet they have the responsibility of assisting me. Almost as if they assist me from backstage in this performance of being in a lifetime. The body that I'm in feels simply like a meat suit, this body is very replaceable, but while I'm in it, they are my backup.

S: Ok, let's leave that scene and move ahead in time to another important day in that same lifetime. Be there now. What do you become aware of?

J: It's the morning of my graduation and I don't want my mother's husband to go. I asked her if she could just not tell him when it was and pretend that she was just going to go out to the store. But she said he would know when she takes a long time and doesn't come back with anything. And I know that if he comes to my graduation that he's going to ruin it; I know that if he goes that he will be absolutely miserable. He will have nothing but negative things to say and drink the whole time and then, drive us home completely drunk afterwards.

S: Tell me more. What happens next?

J: I remember the graduation clearly, especially when they called my name out. I'm not sure what my last name is but my first name is Christina. They called me Christina, but I like to be called Christie.

S: What happened after they called your name out?

J: There was only one person who clapped for me, and it was my mother, and her clapping didn't last very long. Everything about my graduation felt very anticlimactic. It felt like I had wasted my time educating myself, like there was no reward or accomplishment in it. I felt alone in the world, and I felt a lot of resentment when they called my name and I heard only my mother applaud. So many around me had their names called and had choruses of applause and happy messages shouted out at them, and when they called my name, it was very awkward! It was awkward to walk across that stage and take… I was embarrassed to take the diploma.

S: Why were people so hesitant to clap? You said they thought you were weird and just stand offish?

J: They didn't know me. I never let them know me. I didn't want them to get too close and find out about my mother and my stepfather. I didn't want anyone to see the way that he treated us. I didn't want to have to explain that to anyone and I didn't want anyone to see them fighting or the way he attacked us constantly.

S: What else do you notice about your graduation?

J: It looks like the ceremony is in the auditorium in this building. The school is made out of red brick and the windows are black with a crisscross pattern to them with smaller rectangular panes that open at the middle and lift up. They look very old. Outside looks very old too, but the inside has a very (70)s feel to it with the colors and the lockers. It looks like the inside was recently updated in the last couple of years, but not the outside, just the inside. The hallways look very fresh and new, and they don't match the outside.

S: Anything else about your high school years that look interesting?

J: I worked on the school paper. It was the only club that I could find that didn't make me interact with people, and I could stay away from my house later and longer than I was normally expected home. It was a perfect match; it was something I also enjoyed doing. I enjoyed asking questions, but I didn't enjoy having questions asked to me. It worked out very well.

S: What did you do for the school paper?

J: I first started off just doing some basic editing of their articles. The editor would give me a couple of them each week and I would go through them and proofread them as a second set of eyes before they would go to press. I think the name of the paper I work on is called the Sentinel. I see that I obtain a connection after I graduate because of this club that I'm in and they recommend me to a news station nearby. I was excited to work at this news station, but when I start, I see that it is not working in the newsroom, it's working in the mail room. They told me that if I was diligent in my work, and I learn my way around an office then hopefully within a few months they will have an opening and hire me for the news position.

S: What was your job like at this News station?

J: I'm an errand girl. I'm not truly doing any news hunting or investigation. I feel very bottom of the totem pole, very last man in kind of deal. But I see that the news station is called CBS. It appears to be CBS News in Manhattan because I can see the sign as I walk up to it, I can also see the river, and I know that it takes me a while to get to work every day because I have to go all the way across the island to get there.

As Jen painted a much clearer picture of the woman named Christie, I was unaware that she had been contacted by Extra-terrestrials in that lifetime as well. The descriptions of her interaction and intimate details of the life of Christie was what I thought that we would learn more about as we moved forward, but instead, the higher self had other plans for this book.

CHAPTER 2: BUILDING THE SPHINX

As I discuss in my previous book, I had learned that Jen had uncovered this information with a person named Julie once before. What I didn't realize at the time was that there was much more important information that had been uncovered then that had never been released, and so had simmered in the unconscious all these years. As we continued to uncover more of Jen's memories of Christie in the 1970's, surprising information about the Sphinx began to emerge.

S: Ok, let's leave that scene and move ahead in time to another important day. Be there now. What do you become aware of?

J: I remember the first time I started uncovering this information with Julie. I wasn't at her place the first time. I was in the basement of my friend's house where I am living. The house looks like a brownstone, or some kind of building that has a basement to it. It feels like I am in Brooklyn though, or somewhere very close to Brooklyn. I remember when I first met Julie. I had come home, and I was very tired. I'd wanted to go to sleep, and Julie was at the kitchen table with my friend's mother having a glass of red wine. I can see the red wine very clearly. They liked to have red wine every now and then, when Julie would come over. Julie usually came over once a week, and the two of them would catch up. When she saw me coming in and I saw her there was something just…I don't know… there was something very strange between the two of us. She didn't know who I was, and she wanted to be introduced, and we began to talk a little bit. And then my friend's mother said it was time for her to go to sleep because she had to get up very early in the morning. I think she folded clothes for a living, or she worked in a laundry facility where she had to be up very early. But Julie stayed even though my friend's mother went to bed, and we sat there, and she started asking me questions about my life. She asked me about who I was and where I'd come from, and why I was living there. It was a little strange. She was very forward about what she was asking me. I don't feel like it was common for most people to begin asking someone like me questions like that about my life. They would have just been phonier about their conversation in ways, just kind of casually asking who I was. But her questions were very deep and very probing. I felt like I was being very exposed by her questions, and it was almost a little uncomfortable. I think she started to realize that, so she started to explain a little to me about the work she had begun doing. And I thought, well, that seems interesting and once she explained it a little bit better, I wasn't taken aback by everything.

S: How did she explain this work? What kind of work was it?

J: She said that she had come from San Francisco, and that she had spent a lot of time out there. She had done a lot of psychedelics, of all different kinds. Everything that ranged from mushrooms to all the new stuff that people were just beginning to invent. She said she had once been at a point in her life where she wanted to give up and kill herself. But she was too afraid to actively do anything to hurt herself. She realized that she was lacking something, and she didn't know what it was. She was looking for some type of connection, some type of connection to herself and that's when she started using hallucinogens. Through the use of plant medicines, as she called them, she was able to see in a very clear moment what everything really was and how much bigger it was then her, and all the connectivity to it. And the more hallucinogens she did, the more she realized that she was able to start communicating with this other realm that she would go to when she was taking these hallucinogens. After a while she was able to connect on her own without being under the influence of anything. The more she connected on her own without any help the stronger her connection got. And through that practice she was able to gain a new empowered image of herself. She was able to see her past, she was beginning to see parts of her future, and she was able to leave San Francisco and go to New York City and begin a career. She began to do things that she had wanted to do in her life, but always felt very insecure in doing before this experience. And I think that is what I related to the most. I felt very insecure in my life at that point. And the things she was saying to me were very poignant. They were so powerful that it gave me goosebumps thinking of myself in that position. I related to this feeling of wanting something, knowing something was meant to happen in my life and just not knowing what it was; this feeling of not understanding it fully, knowing it had to do with energy and power and healing things in some ways, but having to brush it aside because there was nothing to relate it to and nothing to base it off of.

S: How did she start this process with you? What did she do?

J: The first thing she started with was the candle. There was a candle on the table from when they were drinking wine. And I did say that I was very tired that I did have to go, I did have to get up early in the morning. I said there were things that I needed to do as well. And she said before you leave, stare into this candle with me while I talk. And she started to speak while I was looking straight at the flame of the candle.

S: What did she say? Do you remember?

J: She changed her voice into a very monotonous, slow, and staggered way.

S: Did it sound like hypnosis?

J: Yes. It sounded like hypnosis, it was some form of it, but it sounded like an older person was talking to me, almost like an old shaman was talking to me. As I looked into the candle, I began to feel the water at my feet. It felt like gentle waves beginning to lap up to my ankles and I began to feel the small stones underneath my feet as well, and then, all of a sudden, I remember I felt a wave just slap me. It felt like something just hit me and I snapped out of it real fast.

S: What happened?

J: I think I was just so out of it that I wasn't sure what was really happening to me, so I just said thank you and that I just had to go. But Julie came back the following week. And this time it wasn't as difficult for me to sit and try this out again. I had first tried to avoid her that second evening, but she still sought me out through my friend's mother. She said she wanted to see me and if I was home to ask me to come up. She said she wanted me to try again. She told me to try again, and she said "I want you this time to not feel that fear, or to feel anything, but I just want you to look at the candle and focus only on the candle. Look deep into the flames and don't even pay attention to anything around you." And I did! And I began to see it again, and I began to see even more of it this time.

S: What did you see that time?

J: I opened my eyes that time, like my eyes within my mind, and I saw something for the first time. I saw the ocean in front of me. I saw the ocean from outside my room in my lifetime in Lemuria, from outside the palace. I saw clearly my private beach and the view that I had from there. I could feel the wind and the coolness it would bring as it came off the ocean.

S: Did you know what you were seeing?

J: I knew that it comforted me. At first, all I knew was that it was something that brought me joy when I saw it, but I did not understand what it was and then I looked up and saw the Sphinx.

S: Tell me more about the Sphinx? What did you notice?

J: **As I continued to focus and stare into the candle, I saw it being built.**

S: What did you see?

J: I saw that there were a lot of angular white beams of light moving around in the darkness. It looks like there is a hard rock base that has glints of light within it, the glints look like crystals. The rock base the Sphinx is created on looks like a light orange colored rock that has these little glints of white iridescence within them. That is what the rock looks like that is being dug into. While they dig into this rock it emits a loud sound. It's almost like a helicopter lifting with a whirring sound and a sizzle to it at the end.

S: So, there is a rock that is being dug into?

J: There are these white lights that are being used to dig into it. The tunnels they are digging are very cube like, very boxy and not rounded. They are wide and not cylindrical like other tunnel cities that I have seen before. These tunnels that they are digging under the Sphinx are very angularly cut. It looks like they are taking out the inside of these tunnels and they pulverize it into a dust. It is very dusty as they make this.

S: What are they pulverizing exactly?

J: These lights are just eating away at this rock; it is a very special rock. The rock is very large, very powerful and it was naturally found on the Earth.

S: Do you get a sense as to why this is a powerful rock or what sort of power it has?

J: There are elements within it that are from an asteroid that hit the earth a very long time ago. The asteroid did not leave a crater, but instead imbedded itself within this very large rock. The asteroid was from somewhere else, and it has a very conductive power to it.

S: Do you get a sense of what it can do?

J: It magnetizes, harnesses, and holds this energy if it's directed in the right direction. It has a roughness to it as well, it's not smooth. It feels very rough in some places, but when they cut it with the lasers it comes off as very smooth. It has a power to it though.

S: What type of power?

J: It can hold time. It can hold it in a way that it can stop time as well. It's strange, it can stop time or slow it down as you get closer to it. It's a very conductive and very useful energy. The Sphinx was specifically built on this rock for this reason. The colonizers who came to seed this planet searched and they searched for something that would be a good conduit and they found this.

S: Why did they need a conduit; do you get a sense?

J: Because the information that they were planning on storing in this rock needed to have a generator almost, like a solar panel that keeps the information alive, energized. It keeps the energy from being redundant.

S: Why?

J: They needed it to be kept as a time capsule. They have technology and information that they want to preserve. And this is the best way to store this information. The Sphinx façade is important as well and it is specifically meant to help humans who come across it question what the Sphinx is and where it came from. And it will give those who allow themselves to question this, a sense of belonging to something bigger. It allows them to start thinking outside of their minds. And this was the reason why they chose this structure you call the Sphinx. When the first colonizers came to Earth it was part of their mission to create this vault containing this information, the information of this whole experiment, and this whole creation.

S: Is that information still within?

J: Yes, this information is very alive. **The energy and what is stored within the Sphinx has its own personality, its own field of energy, and its own force.**

S: Could you tell me about that? What is the Sphinx's personality?

J: It is hard to describe. It is very ancient and all knowing. There are more of these structures like the Sphinx that haven't been discovered yet.

S: *Where are they?*

J: Between the middle east and China and also far north towards Russia and Siberia. There is something there as well. There are others that are similar, but they have had other kinds of erosion that have worn away at them, and they sometimes just blend into cliff sides and are not seen for what they are. But there is still a strong physical draw towards them.

S: *What do they look like?*

J: They look very similar in the fact that they were large statues that first presented what would have been one of the apex predators in the area; just like **the Sphinx used to have a jungle cat façade, as that was the apex predator in the area at the time**. They were meant to allow people who encountered these structures to question its purpose and origin. It would give them this curiosity about this alfa creature presented in a rocklike structure. They understood that the apex predators in their area were the most powerful and so they would relate to that, and question what type of power the structure would hold. These structures were very similar to the Sphinx, though the details would change according to the regions.

S: *So, the reason the Sphinx first looked like a jungle cat was because that was the apex predator there?*

J: Yes.

S: *You said that the information is still within the Sphinx. Do you get a sense as to where within the Sphinx it is?*

J: The left paw is where the entrance begins, then it will go down underneath it into the belly, down into these long tunnels that look very boxy. The tunnels go from being very boxy and wide to narrower and more rectangular, and longer.

S: *What is the purpose of the tunnels going from boxy to narrow?*

J: The point is to go from the widening of the mind into this long tunnel and it's supposed to create a sense of transcendence as you go through it. It's not an optical illusion, but this does something to the brain as you travel from this larger, wide space into this narrow longer tunnel.

S: *Would people do this when it was created?*

J: Not very many. It was meant to be preserved for a very long time, until people were wise enough to understand how it works, and wise enough to use the material stored within it for their betterment and not for their destruction.

S: *When is this time?*

J: There is no lock and key in this situation. It is truly opened by the change within the people around it. The raising of their minds, and the changing of the way that they are, will allow access into it. It is only through the mind that you will be able to understand how to enter, and how to see this relic of our origins.

S: Has anyone tried to enter before?

J: Yes, but they were very unsuccessful in finding the information that they thought they were going to find, because they could not perceive it in this dimension, on this level. We are on the wrong level is how it feels. You have to be on the right level to enter.

S: How do you do this?

J: It looks like you must go deeper within yourself. And the answers are very obvious there, very simple and very obvious, but very unperceivable where we are now.

S: Are we going into this level? Moving up? Or no?

J: We are growing in that direction and very strongly moving in that direction. The work that is happening now will be a big push forward for this change of understanding.

S: What will it be like when people are able to enter this place.

J: When they see the truth, and what is held within, and the truth of why we are here, they will understand the truths of what our lives mean and what we have chosen for them to mean. We will begin to live our lives with true purpose and intent.

S: What is the truth of why we are here exactly?

J: **The truth is to understand that we have been here, and placed here, and have been grown here in order to further this experiment.**

S: Is there any other information that you found with Julie about the Sphinx that looks interesting?

J: It is still continuously keeping track of what is going on around it. That is one of the reasons for its shape as well. It continues to keep watch over us and to keep record. Almost like a cat silently watching you without you realizing it, taking in everything around it, and keeping a record. That way when the time is right for this information to be publicly known by the individuals who are awakening to this understanding, there will be a full record of what has happened up until then, and not just a record of a certain point in time. That is one of the reasons for the rock it was built on. The rock was needed to generate this continuous information. It is still observing and sharing our history. There are shared connections from the Sphinx and the information from within it can be sent out almost like the internet. It can travel deep within the Earth and outside the Earth. But when it is shared within the Earth it is shared within something that seems like a gemstone or magnet, but it is something within the Earth that allows this information to travel to many points and for it to come back and be absorbed back into the Sphinx.

S: Can you tell me more about that? **So, the information is coming in through other places and is absorbed into the Sphinx?**

J: Yes, it seems it absorbs information from these beacon-like antennas that are all over the Earth that are feeding this information back to the Sphinx. It's almost as if the Sphinx is a mega hard drive made to store this information so that we can be awakened on a new level once we are ready to receive this, and to be brought to a new point of vibrational harmony with it. When we are ready, we will be able to access the information found within the Sphinx and understand the full picture, and that is the reason for it. But it will be like a download. It will not be someone telling you a story of our history and existence. It will be a very quick download that would change you very drastically because you will fully understand this history for what it really is, and how you are connected to it. You would understand how deep it all has gone, and how much further it will go.

S: How long has it gone on?

J: It is ancient and has gone on for as long as the eye within my mind can see.

S: Tell me more.

J: There is a massive continuum like a figure eight of ebbing and flowing that continuously changes every time we make a decision.

S: When you were watching the Sphinx being built, you said that there were lights that were digging. Were these people or beings who built the Sphinx?

J: They were beings who were not human, or human hybrids, they are something else entirely. They looked like sparkly light beings because they took that intermediate form to come and do this. If you are not on Earth to carry out a mission with the basic early humans than you do not need to take a form. By not taking a form it also allowed them to go back and forth to their home planet. Because when you take a human form, it grounds you here, and keeps you here once you take it.

S: So, they didn't have a human form when they built the Sphinx.

J: It was not necessary, and it was easier for them to build this without the extra weight of a body.

S: How long did it take to build the Sphinx?

J: It takes quite some time. Most of the time was spent creating these long tunnels underneath and connecting them to the right places. The smallest amount of time was spent physically building the jungle cat façade. It seems like there were seven of these light beings who built it. They had been assigned with building the Sphinx and because they had no restrictions, they were able to build intricately without the need to adjust to the conditions of Earth.

S: So, the Sphinx acts like a massive hard drive?

J: A massive hard drive of humanity with the prequel of what led us to come here, of what brought us to Earth, and what we have left behind. It's built into the special rock and there is a large layer of stone that acts like a solar panel to keep this generating and to keep continuously growing this energy and allow more information to come in.

S: Is this type of Sphinx on other planets as well with this same Sphinx-like structure?

J: Yes, there are several. There are some that have been eroded badly, but the basic shape could be outlined on these other planets. Some were planets that were sought out for colonization that didn't work. Some have been forgotten, but there are other planets where it is doing the same thing that we are doing on this Earth.

S: So, this was built before Atlantis, but why was the Sphinx the outpost for Atlantis?

J: In the early days of Atlantis the creator of Atlantis was very adventurous in taking his human slaves and his hybrid slaves with him on his expeditions. He believed that there was much that his ancient ancestors had left behind because he had luckily fallen into a situation where he had found ancient technology. The technology that he had found had been left behind by a much earlier group that had come to set up originally. And he was positive that there was more. He began to search as far as he could while he had the cities and canals being built, the experiments being done. He took many of his human slaves with him as he looked for more technology. He believed that the Sphinx was the furthest point that he could go before there was a massive energy change that he could feel. So, he decided that the Sphinx should be the outpost of Atlantis, a marking factor of where his territory ended and began.

S: Did you work with Julie a lot to uncover this information?

J: We did. I would come home in the evening from work or school, and it would be about the same time that my friend's mother would have to go to bed. After saying goodnight to her, Julie would stay with me for about an extra hour once a week just working with me and uncovering all this information. But after a while I would go and meet her at her place after I got out of work because her house was a little closer to the station. The information came out of me very quickly.

CHAPTER 3: SURPRISING INFORMATION ABOUT MARS

It appeared that there was a lot of information that Julie and Christie had uncovered besides the information that Jen and I had retrieved about Atlantis and Lemuria. Below is interesting information about Mars.

S: *What other information did you both uncover?*

J: There was so much because it all came out of me so quickly once I would stare at the candle. It was as if images just flooded to me. Sometimes they would be confusing at first. I remember finding information about Mars in our sessions. As I said, there was so much that came out of me all of a sudden that I never processed and it was very confusing to me consciously, so I pushed this information out of my conscious memory.

S: *Tell me about what you had uncovered about Mars?*

J: It didn't look at all like it does now. It looked more alive, it had water, land, and it looked like a very active planet. But there was an explosion that happened very close to Mars, and when the explosion happened, it made life on Mars very difficult. But before this destruction there was a lot of life on Mars as Mars was a planet that was sought out for colonization.

S: *So, what happened?*

J: The explosion near Mars created a blanket of smoke around the planet that suffocated everything and that is why it looks the way it does now.

S: *What type of beings used to live on Mars?*

J: They look a lot like people, but I don't think they're humans.

S: *What makes you say that?*

J: The beings that went to Mars to colonize seem to look like they are from another part of the Universe, but at this point Earth looked different as well, and at that time Earth wasn't inhabitable yet. The Earth was still too hot, and the atmosphere on Earth was poisonous.

S: *So, what happened?*

J: The explosion near Mars created a blanket of smoke around the planet that suffocated everything and threw their development off course. The beings on Mars seemed to have been a very early grouping of beings and not the same grouping of beings who came to colonize Earth. This destruction on Mars happened much earlier and was destroyed before Earth was colonized, like I said. It predates that. The beings that came to Mars had the intention of setting up alternate civilizations to their own and were looking to create an outpost. This happened so long ago when conditions on Mars were different than they are now. The conditions on Mars were more hospitable, and the conditions on Earth were not, and that is why Earth wasn't an option. Earth was very early in its development, and Mars looked very much like Earth did at that point. The colonization of Mars went on for a while, but from what I remember uncovering with Julie was that it was something in Mars's nearby orbit that exploded. As I focus closer in on this memory, I see that when it exploded it was such a massive explosion that it threw off the orbit of Mars. Because of this, Mars became clouded with a blanket of smoke, and it also started to get much colder as the skies became covered with a dark ash. This ash was very thick and high up into the atmosphere, not down below near the surface, and this ash covered the planet before it then started to kill off everything. It looks as though there were issues with their governance before this happened.

S: Tell me about that.

J: There was something very tumultuous happening between these colonists there, some fighting it looks like. I can't see exactly what it was, but they were able to build very sophisticated things because they used the natural resources that were available to them on Mars. They had built into the rock, and they had many underground tunnels within the planet. But even the tunnels couldn't be sustained after this explosion.

S: Why not?

J: Life could not come back to the planet after that.

S: Why did they have a tunnel system?

J: They used the tunnels for transport, especially for the crops that they were growing there.

S: How did they do that?

J: They would send the crops through these long tunnels underneath and it was easier to transport them that way. And many of these people went into the tunnels after the explosion, smoke, and cold happened, but they couldn't survive. They couldn't grow enough food, or get the right conditions, and as that planet began to die some of those beings were removed, were saved. The beings on Mars were able to send off a beacon to their original planet to get help for the survivors, but because it took a while for the help to come, they were few in numbers when help did finally come for them.

S: How did the help come?

18

J: Help came from the other planet by ship. The planet was signaled through a series of very cloudy white crystals and through a very large electronic motherboard on Mars. The crystals were placed in three different places on this rectangular looking large device the size of a keyboard piano. Maybe about four feet long.

S: What was life like on Mars before this destruction?

J: It was very simple. There wasn't much of anything, but there was also no native population on Mars for these newcomers to mix with.

S: What did the people on Mars look like?

J: They look like they are taller and greyer. Like tall greys, but with more bug like features to them. Their mouths look like a praying mantis as did their legs, because they were bent at an angle. They also had this extra growth around the mouth.

S: Did they eat food?

J: They were vegetarian in nature. They grew certain crops that were very high in chlorophyll or something green that nourished them.

S: Where did those beings go after Mars was destroyed?

J: They were transported back to their home planet that was very far away. It is about thirteen million light years away, but I don't understand that measurement. Their home planet looks larger than Earth, like twice the size of Earth, but it also looks very dense. Dense as in there is a lot of them there and that is why they were looking to set up these colonies. Mars was not the only one that they set up, there were other colonies set up in other areas of the Universe that were more successful.

S: Do you get a sense if there are any people walking the Earth right now that were on Mars when this destruction happened?

J: Many of them have come to Earth now because **this is the time where we are uncovering the history of Mars.** These are the early days of understanding that there was a colony there. There are many people that have memories of living there.

S: What are their memories like?

J: Some people remember feeling very stuck, very trapped, very unable to do anything themselves. Many of the souls that perished on Mars are returning now with that same feeling echoed in this current life. However, there are many opportunities for them to confront this past and to move away from it. It is very important to those people from Mars to remember this legacy that they left there. It is important that they begin to see signs of this old civilization that was left that had turned to dust.

S: What do you mean by that? What do these people need to see?

J: Many have a deep desire to see the colony of Mars rebuilt.

S: Why is it important for them to see this?

J: It is important for them on many levels. It may be the most important thing that they need for their ascension because once they understand that they really were there, and that this devastation happened to them, then it will stop interfering with their next lives.

S: How do these people go about doing this? Just through a regression?

J: That is one of the most successful ways to do it, is to do these regressions, but many of those who need this information will be subconsciously led to this book and it will trigger that memory within them.

S: How do people know if they lived during that time of Mars's destruction?

J: Many dream of that life, or they have fleeting memories or images of it. Reading this will not only give them this understanding, but it will also give them the ability to look further into that life. As they take a closer look within themselves, they can see what happened during that time, what happened to this colony, and see why it is still haunting them -the traumatic effect of being left in that colony, left to die. Many of these people are looking to rebuild this colony on Mars now.

S: Tell me more about that.

J: It looks very structured. There are already structures in place. It will be populated soon enough, and humans will be there.

S: Tell me more.

J: This will happen in our current lifetimes.

S: What will happen exactly?

J: Many of the people who will go to Mars and colonize it are the same people who lived there before. These are old souls who need to finish something unfinished. And not everyone who is there will be able to go back at first but everyone who was there, who is in a physical body, a physical reality now, will feel that pull towards it if they are one of those people. They will feel that they will relate and understand that this is part of them. They will feel that they were there and that this happened to them. They were left abandoned on that planet and in the aftermath of this massive destruction, of what looks like a collision in space, they remember in many ways the severity of needing to stay alive and not knowing if they would ever be rescued. We will see the beginning of this colony in our life.

S: What kind of collision was this that caused that destruction?

J: An asteroid hit something. I can't tell if it was a moon or a small planet. Something spherical was hit by something that was very long and cigar shaped. It feels like it was a dense metal that was floating through space like a rocket almost. Just this huge, long asteroid.

S: *Was there a purpose or plan for this collision, or was it an accident?*

J: Nothing is ever an accident, but I don't see the reason for it. However, there is reasoning to everything. While it may not be the reason that makes the most sense to you or the reason that feels the fairest.

S: *Is it possible that this could happen to Earth?*

J: Down the road towards the end of Earth's existence this could be an issue, but for now no.

S: *How many star systems are there?*

J: Infinite.

S: *Does a person's soul go to different star systems, or do they stay in this one?*

J: It is up to the individual soul. Souls have all been to many and will continue to go to many over the course of their experiences. But some get stuck in a star system.

S: *How do they get stuck?*

J: They make a plan and never finish it. No matter what the beings/ species are, we all have similar developmental goals and ways to evolve that we are all trying to achieve no matter where we are, or where we come from. And even though we are all from different planets, different star systems and different realms, we are still all part of that same source. Even though there can be a difference in appearance or history, it all comes back to that same singular golden glowing orb of oneness that is everything.

S: *Where did that source come from?*

J: It didn't come from anywhere. It is infinite and very much something that has always been, and we continue to come from it and return to it.

S: *Is there a star language?*

J: When you hit a certain point, the language is telepathic and completely in the mind. It is less a conversation, and more of an openness to understanding one's intention. The conversation becomes very limited when you have to speak in words.

S: *Tell me more about the way that other beings speak telepathically to one another.*

J: There are many different ways, but sometimes there is touching involved that transmits energy and understanding. When two beings touch each other, it can change the other's energy and allows them to experience the other's understanding. It is quiet because it doesn't have unsophisticated meaningless conversation.

S: *What do they talk about?*

J: They often communicate with each other about what they have learned and what information they have gathered. Many times, they talk about their interactions with humans.

S: *Oh, tell me more about that.*

J: They have to keep tabs on the humans and interact with them for many reasons but one of the reasons is so that they can understand how their evolvement is progressing. Human evolution is important to all the beings as a whole, because they are affected by whatever humanity chooses.

S: *How? Tell me more?*

J: We are all interlinked in this system.

CHAPTER 4: RECOVERING MEMORIES WITH JULIE

When Jen and I uncovered the information about the end of days in Atlantis and Lemuria, I was often curious about the other time periods of these places as well. Below is interesting information about another time period in what is known as Atlantis.

S: Is there anything different about the information that you received with Julie then and the information you're getting now?

J: I was able to get more of it then, and it has been a bit halted in this lifetime because they have slowed it down on purpose.

S: Do you get a sense why?

J: It has been halted slightly to ensure that it wouldn't be too overwhelming this time. Because in that previous lifetime as Christie, it was apparent that it was. Especially overwhelming to receive it all at once. So, they have slowed the process down in my current life as Jen. It looks like it was less than six months from the time that I met Julie to the time that I died. Between six months to ten at the absolute most.

S: Is there any other information that you uncovered with Julie that seems important?

J: **Yes. I received information about someone named Thoth or Three, as I feel he was called.** The information I received about Atlantis and Lemuria with Julie, and all these things that you and I uncovered about these lands, were the same. Julie and I uncovered the same information about my lifetime as a queen in Lemuria who was taken as a prisoner by the Atlanteans. I remember we uncovered the same information about the virus they had, the experiments and the vaccine experiments, but there was just a lot more about Thoth/Three that I feel was important to us then.

S: What did you receive about Thoth/ Three?

J: That he/it was around in the aftermath of Atlantis guiding, trying to find a way for people to not recreate what had just happened in Atlantis. Thoth/Three had come back again in some reincarnated form to this island with an emerald sea in front of it. There were people at war and Three intervenes on behalf of these two warring factions on this island. Three tries to teach reason to these people, it tries to reeducate them before they destroy each other. But Three is ultimately unsuccessful.

S: Why do you say it when talking about Three instead of he or she?

J: When I say he or she it doesn't feel correct. The being named Three feels like an it, or they.

S: What did Three look like?

J: Three could shape shift and take different forms based on what was most comfortable for people around it to see. In this version that I see from my memories uncovered with Julie it takes the appearance of a masked being. It almost reminds me of the masks that the people wore during the plaque. It takes this form to look almost like a God to try to convince people to behave themselves and stop hurting each other.

S: So, this was after Atlantis was destroyed?

J: Yes. After the fall of Atlantis there was a visit by what you would call Thoth, or Three, to this community. But Thoth/Three is an extra-terrestrial. It is not an incarnation of a human.

S: Where does Three come from?

J: It looks like it had come from my home planet, very far away. Even though Three had come to try to talk sense to people, he was unsuccessful, and the Emerald Island was destroyed. But during this other worldly intervention, Three gives these communities information that they write down. The information it shared was very important for those communities and were the keys they needed to move forward and evolve.

S: What kind of information is it?

J: I can't understand it, it looks very squiggly. It looks very angular with different kinds of angular patterns to it. It looks very familiar, but I just can't read it.

S: The information was to help these people?

J: It is meant to help people evolve. There were simple rules to follow that would help their society prosper, and that is what he presented to them.

S: Why didn't it work?

J: There was too much of a divide within the minds of people. There was too much of a divide between this divine feminine and masculine that had happened as a result of the destructions of Lemuria and Atlantis. People did not want to focus on working together, instead they were more focused on overcoming one another with a male domination. We're seeing another incarnation of this Three now. There is other worldly intervention here, with us now. We are seeing it happen. We are given this chance again and we are more aware this time! We are more awake to see past ourselves and see the larger picture rather than continuously ignore these teachings that this soul brings to us. We are not ignoring it this time.

S: How has that soul been reincarnated in this time period? Is it in a body?

J: Yes, possibly, but I cannot get a clear picture of where this Three is. But I feel that it has also been incarnated in many earlier settlements as well when there were people looking to destroy. And Three comes and steps in to help us work through things rather than destroy ourselves. It shows up amongst us now more like an earth power, and earth presence, and possibly in many individuals at this time.

S: Let's move ahead in time to another session that you have with Julie. What do you become aware of?

J: I had remembered coming to Earth for the first time as the commander of an extra-terrestrial ship and I remember uncovering many things with Julie. During one session, I remember we also saw other time periods during Atlantis, not just the time when I lived there as a prisoner. I remember I saw small pyramids all around Atlantis, not large ones, smaller pyramids that seem to be dotted through their landscape where they live. The pyramids had within them these clear crystals that didn't have color, but some were very opaque. The clearer ones were the stronger ones. They look like wands but both ends have a sharp point to them, and they were suspended inside these pyramids with what looks like a small metal object. The metal was in the shape of a UFO, a roundish shape that comes to a point at the end, inside the pyramid. That was what the shape of the metal that held the crystals looked like. They were not donut shaped but they were round on top and pointy at the ends. And inside of these devices were crystals that were placed onto what looks like a two-pronged metal holder. And from this a great white light came out of these pyramids. It wasn't hot, just very bright. They were very powerful, and it didn't feel like electricity was coming out of them, but some other type of immense power. The power from these pyramids was so great that you could feel it without being there.

S: What was this power used for?

J: It was used to power Atlantis.

S: Can you tell me more about this power?

J: It came from an energy grid system that was created very early on and it was dug out along these canals when the originator of Atlantis structured his empire. This energy grid had been upgraded and repaired over the years, but it existed and remained intact for thousands and thousands of years. It was compatible with the rings of water that went around the capital of Atlantis as well and the water and the energy system worked together.

S: How do they work together?

J: The rings of water, or moats acted as a barrier to stop the crystal energy system from backfiring or misfiring. The moats around Atlantis were also used so that the whole city would not be destroyed if there was a backfire, because the water would protect the next outer ring. The energy would stay within the ring and the moats had a barrier effect to them. This feels somewhat similar to the way the red crystals worked back in Lemuria. The energy from our red crystals in Lemuria only went up to the water's edge.

S: How does it seem similar?

J: These systems in Lemuria and Atlantis were both built very early on and were built into the framework of the island. The island that was my home (Lemuria) had an element of protection to it when it came to the health of my people. And the Atlanteans did not have that because they had a different type of crystal. The crystals that I see in these pyramids in Atlantis worked in many ways and it seems that it keeps the Atlanteans very busy, and I want to say intelligent, but there is a better word for it.

S: So, these crystals in Atlantis keep them busy and intelligent?

J: Yes, but the crystals that they have there aren't the same as the ones that we had in Lemuria, so the effect is different and the Atlanteans didn't have that immunity from disease like we did. But their crystals have a special effect to them where it keeps the Atlanteans very busy, it keeps them thinking in a very different way. It creates a very logical thinking process. It fosters scientific development, and these crystals allow their brains to focus on technology and progression. By being near this energy and absorbing this energy into your body it would work with your natural energy to create a very scientific person. It appears that these crystals kept them isolated within this bubble because of this energy.

S: So, if you were to set up the same set of crystals now, could you foster that ability now?

J: It would have to be set up with the same grid work that it had in Atlantis.

S: When the founder of Atlantis set up the crystals this way how did he know to do this?

J: This was also done on his home planet, and it was part of the founder of Atlantis's training before he came to Earth. Some of his training involved how to build, how to create these systems, and how to create these lines under the ground that could help power things. It was all taught to him. And that is why he was a member of this crew. He was intending to structure the new cities, the new colonies that we were building on Earth.

S: Did you have this knowledge as well when you were a commander of an extra-terrestrial ship?

J: I had a general knowledge of it, but I was not a specialist in this area. My area of specialty and what I had been focused on was the regeneration of the hybrid children. And that was what I was intended to focus on during that journey to Earth.

S: Could you tell me more about your specialty?

J: It looks that they had trained me for many years alongside several others who would go to other places on different journeys to Earth at nearly the same time as myself. We were part of a class that divided up and we would each have our own separate missions and our own teams and over the years I had risen through the ranks and into a higher position acquiring my own team. And this was needed on some of these missions. Someone who could command a ship and also have intricate knowledge of several areas that would be useful in setting up a colony. And I was chosen early on to specialize in this. The information I learned, and my specialties were very different from what I had grown up to understand, but my people had very advanced knowledge of how things were going to have to work on Earth and I became acquainted with that over time.

S: What kind of knowledge did you have to become acquainted with?

J: I didn't have a full understanding of what it was really like to actually live on Earth. I didn't understand what eating or even walking was. It was actually very confusing for me to understand at first. We didn't walk very much on my home planet. We would float at this point of our development, but perhaps it is more of a mechanical device that allows us to do this and to levitate almost. There was no heaviness to the body in walking and moving when I lived on my planet. You felt like you were gliding lightly, and you wouldn't have that heavy feeling like you do when you are walking on Earth. That was one of the strangest things that was different and hard to get used to, but there were many other things. I wasn't aware at all of these strange things about Earth until we began our training. And then during my training I came to understand how important our journey to Earth was going to be in the continuation of our kind. I understood that I was going to become a different person once I left this home planet and became an earthling. And I came to this planet Earth knowing that I would leave myself behind in many ways, becoming a new being.

S: Did you plan on staying on Earth for a long time?

J: That was part of the mission and the training. It was intended to be a long-term journey.

S: Had you done that before?

J: This was the only time in that lifetime.

S: When you were living as a commander did you have memories of your other lifetimes?

J: No, I didn't. I wasn't in touch with those in that lifetime as a commander because they had been specifically blocked to allow for this new journey, this new passage. But looking at this lifetime from a different perspective I see that that was not my first lifetime in any way. I was destined to go there **because in a previous lifetime I was one of the beings who set the ley lines down on Earth.**

CHAPTER 5: LEY LINES

What can only be described as the Earth's underground superhighways built by extra-terrestrials, Ley Lines have always fascinated me, and so I asked Jen for more information on their origin and infrastructure. As follows is Jen's recount as commander of this fascinating extra-terrestrial mission.

S: Tell me about that. **When did you set the ley lines down?**

J: The ley lines were set before we started colonizing in Antarctica. I was one of the first to go there and start structuring.

S: How were the ley lines set up?

J: It was done with a mental and physical combination. It wasn't just a physical thing that needed to be done. There was a large amount of mental work involved to focus this energy into doing what it was supposed to do, but the Earth looked very different then. It didn't look like it looks now. It was very red, very hot and very wet, like a hot, red, wet heat kind of. It was also salty and almost like it was burning a bit.

S: How were you able put the ley lines down with it being hot? Did the heat affect you?

J: No. We were able to use a type of equipment that focuses deep within the Earth as it goes down. It looked like a giant needle that tapped into the different types of…it's not a metal or a rock, but an element that's in the Earth and it created points there. So, if I picked a point that I knew would be a good beneficial point for a civilization to start on, I would mark it off there. Then we would stick this massive device into this area, and it would almost in a magnetizing way connect it to this point, and it would create a line, like a magnetic grid, underneath the Earth that would align to these points. And we were able to go to several different places to lay these down. This took quite a while to do. We would use two devices to connect these lines and points, one to begin and two on the other end. And you could use these two to communicate with each other. This would allow these ley lines to join together and not only communicate through these large lines but communicate underneath the ground. These lines could stretch for thousands of miles. The distance was not an issue with them it was just making sure that we found the right spots to pinpoint them to.

S: How did you find the right spots?

J: Looking at Earth from above we would map them out as far as we could understand of what we knew the Earth changes would be over the next couple hundreds of thousands of years. We would locate and map out the most appropriate places to put civilizations knowing that the Earth would go through these changes. And we looked for areas that were of higher ground, areas that we knew people would be able to find that also had some kind of sustenance and fresh water. It was also mapped out for humans to be able to find these places, to be drawn to them, magnetized towards them. In that way we would not lose our colonies and we would also be able to keep track of them. The humans we seeded were in many ways in tune to this energy within these ley lines. And since the humans would be drawn to these spots, they would always find their way back to us.

S: How are humans in tune with these ley lines exactly?

J: It seems that we designed them to be this way, while we were designing the system. This allowed us in our earlier days of colonizing to keep track of the humans in this large world that we created where there weren't as many humans as there are now. It helped us keep track of our hybrids knowing that they had these energy sources underground to guide them as well. We knew that since the human would be drawn to these ley lines, they would always congregate close to these points and because of this we were able to keep better track of where they were and not lose as many of them.

S: Were there any other reasons for the ley lines?

J: The ley lines were also created to have a system designed for our beings to come to this planet and colonize it and give the colonizers easy access throughout the Earth because they would no longer have the ability to fly or to easily go to the next colony. Through the ley lines they were also able to communicate within colonies and travel. In the absence of all our technology, if all else fails, we would have access to an underground system prepared to protect us and guide us and to allow us to remember the keys back to our origins, of why we were there.

S: Can a person now use these ley lines?

J: Humans are still tuned to these ley lines and that's why they're drawn to them. It's part of our human existence and our genetics. Some who are purer in their energy are able to connect into them and use this energy, though it's not being utilized to its full potential in the way that it can be.

S: How can you use this energy within the ley lines now?

J: You can use this energy to refresh the body with it.

S: How?

J: By coming into contact with the ley lines and meditating while you are in proximity to them, and mentally allowing the energy of these lines to absorb into your body. It has a large effect on the body, almost like a resetting, a refreshing. It entirely changes the perspective of a person, and it gives them a boost of this specific energy in order to help them with what they need.

S: Do you have to be close to a ley line to do this or can you set the intention for this energy to come into you?

J: You need to be close to it in order to do this and that is what is special about them; they have this power that magnetizes humans towards them.

S: What are vortexes then?

J: They were the ancient transport devices that were used by the early settlers in these pinpointed spots that connected the ley lines that allowed these early settlers to transport themselves into different colonies throughout the Earth. One example would be the stone circles at Stonehenge.

S: Does this transport system still work?

J: The system that allowed colonists to go back and forth between many of these old colonies has been broken down over time, but the process of using them to enter into a different dimension is still active.

S: Do people still travel through these unexpectedly? Is this like what we learned previously about the Bermuda triangle?

J: Yes, there are many missing person reports that were never solved because of these things.

S: Were there ley lines on your home planet?

J: There were.

S: Was the history of your planet like Earth? Did they start the same?

J: Looking back it seems similar. Though the ley lines on Earth have a golden tone to them and ours on my home planet have a white light to them. They are different but the structure and the purpose were still the same.

S: Do you always do things slightly differently when coming to a new planet or do you try to keep things the same?

J: There is always a small amount of difference instituted in order to create variance and variety. Doing the same and repetition has its benefits, but it doesn't allow for progression.

S: So, the founder of Atlantis set up these pyramids. Were there any other healing technologies that ancient Atlanteans used?

J: There were, but those were things that were at a different time in Atlantis than during my time there. They were at a much earlier time, a time within the middle where things were a bit simpler. There was a time in Atlantis when people had overthrown their oppressors and were living a closer life to what they wanted, compared to where they had started off with their genetic mutations and experiments. They had finally reached a point somewhere in the middle of the history of Atlantis that allowed for them to overthrow their rulers, and the peace they found was what they were looking for. They used crystals for many different purposes and there was a brief time of healing. But it isn't the same healing we had in Lemuria. It is a different kind of healing.

S: What kind of healing was it?

J: The people of Atlantis were very traumatized. They had been through so much; they had been willingly put through so much. And the healing that occurs through these crystals is a healing of the soul. There was a removing of these chains, of removing this identity of being someone's possession and of removing this idea that you are nothing more than a drone or a worker. It was a revolution of healing through these new crystals that allowed people to reaffirm their identity as a person rather than a possession, and that is where the healing began for them. This healing lasts for quite some time and then I see it just plummets. There is a moment where everything just starts to go crazy.

S: What happened?

J: There is just a point in Atlantis that everyone gets to where they are all healed and have released the oppression, and then the individual identities that they have gained from this new way of life begin to conflict with each other.

S: Tell me about that.

J: Some developed the need to have a superiority in this newfound identity. They stop desiring this comradery or this ability to all be together as one. They start to associate togetherness with being workers, with being slaves. And these ideas of superiority create the tiered society that they begin. They start competing amongst each other and it brings people to a very bad place. They start to become very self-centered to where they don't care about other people anymore.

S: Why does this consistently happen throughout history over and over again?

J: It is part of the human condition that we are eventually meant to graduate from and that is why we continuously see it over and over again. We continuously fail to overthrow it, to release ourselves from this pattern. However, people now are learning to shed their false identity that they have created for themselves. And in doing so there is freedom. It is the freedom that we have been seeking for so long.

CHAPTER 6: THE HISTORY OF EGYPT

As Jen recovered more of her memories with Julie interesting information about Atlantis and the history of Egypt emerged.

S: When you were working with Julie, did you ever uncover other planets that appeared to have the same technology that Atlantis did? I've had many clients recount other lifetimes on other planets that seemed to have this same technology.

J: Yes. That is because it is all derived from the same source.

S: So, there were many planets with this technology? Just like Atlantis?

J: There were many planets colonized by what I would call the Red Planet and the Blue Planet before Earth was colonized. There are many others out there that are like us, but they are very far away from us.

S: Do these other planets with the same technology that Atlantis had also have situations where they are mutating people as well or no?

J: Some. There are many different variables. Some of these other planets have had similar outcomes and some have avoided these situations all together. But the ones who have had lives that mimic those you have seen on Atlantis all seem to end the same way. They all seem to have these cataclysmic endings to these colonies that become very technologically advanced.

S: Was there a golden age in Atlantis?

J: Yes, at an earlier time in Atlantis. There was an earlier point in Atlantis's history, way before the final years, but after the city was built, and after the founder of Atlantis, who had designed the city, had lost his crystals. When he lost his red crystals, things were left to just develop with what technology he had without the crystals and people began to use their minds in ways that they had not been able to use them while they were imprisoned. They had been repressed from using their gifts, from using their abilities. And the founder of Atlantis had in many ways mutated so many of them. He had cloned, mutated, and used all kinds of animal DNA, in order to create these efficient workers to build his empire and to defend him. And when he lost all of it and that was gone, a short golden age is what developed afterwards. There was a utopia almost of high technology, and freedom, and this movement together of these people who had been constantly oppressed and forced to not recognize who they were. They were free from continuously slaving away for a system that had entrapped them. They had gotten to a point where they were moving in the right direction and then there is an energetic mistake that is made. It was very powerful, devastating, and it turned them into a dust, like an evaporation almost. From what I can see it looks like a light that just kind of goes all over in 360 sphere outwards from one source that looks like a golden lit orb.

S: So, this was a cataclysm on Atlantis before the final one?

J: Yes, it was a very big energetic cataclysm. It puts them back very far. It puts them back to a very basic time where they have to rebuild their society and it takes them a very long time to build it back up to what they once had. It just destroys their energy systems and all their circuitry. It really affects their development for a very long time, a long time before we have the reign that allows for the meeting of Lemuria and Atlantis together.

S: How long after this did both cultures meet?

J: At least 5,000 years.

S: How many times was Atlantis destroyed or almost destroyed?

J: The first time was in the beginning of Atlantis when it was being seeded and then was abandoned. There was a terrible fight amongst the colonizers and the feelings of heaviness, regret and remorse were too great. So those colonizers abandoned what they had started and left their technology. So then if you count that, the extra-terrestrial that crash landed and destroyed the lifestyle of those living there, that would be the second, the third and then the fourth. But the actual explosions of Atlantis were the minor one that caused much land destruction, and the major one that caused the sinking of it.

S: Can you tell me more about the minor destruction?

J: The minor one shook the framework up enough to allow for an easier way to ultimately destroy it the second time. It created something that looked almost like lightning underground. It had created these cracks that had begun to unsettle the continent of Atlantis. It began the uprooting process of Atlantis. From what I could see with Julie, Atlantis had a very long history from the time the first ET settler goes there to when it ends. It had many ups and downs and many different leaders that I can see. Some were very beautiful and good, but there was always a basic understanding that the Atlanteans originated and had ancestors who were actually hybrid slaves created by an alien. That was always in the background of their consciousness. They felt sometimes superior because of it and sometimes degraded because of it.

S: After the fall of Atlantis the last one, were there hybrids who started ancient Egypt?

J: The Cat People, people who were born with cat-like side effects from the vaccine in Atlantis, were the hybrids who began a lot of the highly advanced spiritual concepts in ancient Egypt. They continued and spread a lot of beneficial and helpful information for some time until their society became chaotic and violent. Then a group of men realized that they could ban together and reclaim this superiority and domination. This group of men felt that the gold that the Cat People wore around their heads and wrists was simply something that they could do as well. This group felt that they could use the devices that the Cat People had in the same way, and they could use these devices to control others as well. But once this group of men had killed all of the Cat People, they saw that they not only didn't have the same abilities as the Cat People, but that they didn't know how to use these devices. So, this group of control hungry men just faked it and were able to convince people of their power and were able to finally control them.

S: What happened after that?

J: The threat of violence was so great that no one would speak up against this group of power-hungry men and it begins this slow regression of humankind. It began this dominant vs vulnerable species within this group of humans, one that would need protection and one that would need to be the protector, and it created a very deep imbalance.

S: When did Ancient Egypt and the Pharaohs begin?

J: Not to long after Egypt was overthrown by these men. For a few generations the control group spread out as the areas grew in population. And the controllers settled in two different parts, one in the North and one in the South and they are about to start fighting with each other when one man is able to bring them both together. It is still a very violent brutal place, but they began to create a rebirth of Atlantis as they try to reclaim Atlantis even though the actual Atlantis had already been destroyed at this point.

S: Tell me more about that.

J: This man that unites the North and South suggests that they are all supposed to reclaim Atlantis, that they were supposed to bring it back, that this was their right. He claimed that they had unfairly lost their power, their land, their leader. These were the legends that were passed down after they had destroyed many of the Cat People, and it just looks like these ideas just get out of control.

S: How does it go out of control?

J: It allows for power to be entirely corrupted and creates a society of people who are afraid of each other, but who must carry on and continuously do labor and keep feeding this system that was created. It's no longer about a community and providing for one another and making sure everyone has what they need. It becomes very competitive and very classist and very divided. And this is the reclaiming of Atlantis. They convinced each other that they were taking back what was theirs, that it was their promise land, their birthright, that it belonged to them.

S: Why did they say it was Atlantis? Did they have any leftover technology?

J: They didn't, but they had very vague ideas from these lessons, rituals, and teachings of the survivors from Atlantis and the Cat People. And these ideas, teachings and rituals that had been passed down were interpreted differently based off of what the controlling group wanted.

S: Were they similar? What kind of rituals were they?

J: They were not the same, they were based on worshiping the Sun. They were based on the connection to it and the white light that came from it. They were looking to reconnect with the power of the Sun, and they wanted to reharness and create this white light that was the source of creation. I feel that was their major goal, to get back that aspect of what they had lost; this power that was given to them that was taken away.

S: What kind of power did they have before?

J: They understood that there had been energies that were used to create these major cities in Atlantis and these hybrid communities, and they wanted this technology again.

S: So, they thought the technology made them powerful?

J: Yes, they thought the technology would allow them to build empires and with these empires they thought that they could build prosperity, wealth, and success.

S: Tell me more about the power of the Sun in Atlantis.

J: The sun charged all of their devices and had an intricate part to play in their technology. They were able to take sunlight and use it through these crystals that they had within the pyramids, and it refracted off of the crystals and created energy.

S: What did the controlling group that was interested in the reclamation of Atlantis feel about the Sun?

J: They felt the need to worship it, even though that was not the point. They felt that it was a God self, and they began to make sacrifices to it as if that would do something. But the Sun is the Sun and that wasn't necessary. A bunch of misconceptions began to surround the very basic understandings of what this ancient power was. And it becomes something it wasn't and never was. They make it up to be this complicated thing with all this symbolism but it's actually just simply the Sun, but after the grid system was destroyed, we couldn't tap into it the way we once did after the fall of Atlantis. There were also highly developed mental abilities that were needed in order to fully understand and tap into this power as well.

S: How did the actual Atlanteans tap into it?

J: During this time when these Atlanteans used this Sun technology, they had more of an understanding of who they really were and that enabled their powers of the mind. Since most do not have that understanding any longer these mental powers have grown very weak, lethargic, and very diluted.

S: How do we enable these powers again?

J: It is one of the reasons for this book. Many who will read this will start to cast off the shadows that they alone had cast on their own abilities. It is also happening through ET contact and is one of the reasons you are seeing so many alien abductions happening around us over the last twenty years. These are intentional in order to change our programing, to allow us to go back to a time when we had certain mental abilities. However, the new children are different.

S: How are the children different?

J: Their DNA is different than ours, it has changed. They have already been programmed back towards the opening in the mind that connects us to our origins and how to use these ancient abilities we were once gifted with.

S: When you say new children, what ages do you mean?

J: About ten and under (this is April 2021) and some are older than that, but not all.

S: Are we headed in that new direction then, where we will understand these things?

J: In the last ten years much has been done to make sure that the next generation of children will be very different. They have been programed differently, and much effort has been made to begin to open their minds very slowly again, but in the right direction, to awaken these abilities once more.

S: Could you tell me more about the Pharaohs in ancient Egypt? Why would the Pharaohs marry their sisters? Is that true?

J: For some it was. Once Egypt was a unified kingdom many generations down the road, the in breeding between families began to happen because they felt that the power must be maintained within the family in order to continue having hybrid children, the special children.

S: Were the Pharaohs hybrid children?

J: There were a few that had this recessive gene.

S: Did they look any different than other humans?

J: They did. Some of these children were the great, great grandchildren of some of the escapees of Atlantis that did carry these things deep within their genetics. They had reestablished an order of superiority over the indigenous humans because of this.

S: How did they look different?

J: They had very long and bony faces, their bodies also would look longer and more angular instead of muscular and built. They dominated people in the way that they looked different, not in the way that they looked aggressive or powerful in physique. They had a very different facial structure sometimes, more catlike, or aloof as well sometimes, because they had some of the recessive genes that were passed down through the ages from Atlantis.

S: Were they really keeping the power within that bloodline if they married brother and sister?

J: It wasn't necessary to do so, it was a misunderstanding. It caused more harm than good with the mixing of the blood like that. It led to lots of insanity that only complicated the matters. And King Tutankhamun was a good example.

S: Tell me more about him.

J: Not only was his health not very good due to the incestuous relationships throughout generations, but his life was also very confusing for him. It seems that he had issues walking and some other issue with his heart possibly. He looked like he was a very anxious child, that he was constantly worried because of his mother's incessant worries that people were trying to kill him. His mother had told him that people were coming for him and that he must tap back into this ancient power and use this power in order to protect him and her.

S: Was he able to do that?

J: I don't think so. I did not remember that when I was uncovering this memory with Julie. It looked like he wasn't able to do such a thing. He tried and did everything right that he thought he should do, he had the knowledge. He understood that he was from the stars, and he understood his power, he just could not connect back to it.

S: Did you see why he couldn't connect?

J: He just didn't have the ability, but he could tap into other things, just not what he wanted to.

S: What could he tap into?

J: He was able to see the past, but only very mundane things. Things that were not very interesting or very useful. He was often correct, but it wasn't anything that they could use in any way. And the past that he could see was never very far back. He could see up until right before Egypt became what it is. He could see to the beginning of Egypt after the second Sphinx was destroyed, but he couldn't see back to the end of Atlantis. The people knew what Atlantis was, but they could not tap back into the energy there and that was what they were trying to do with him. Anything else he came up with was not useful, but it was still something.

S: Did he ever marry?

J: He did marry his sister, but it wasn't for very long and he wasn't very happy with it either. He was very young and uninterested then.

S: Did he have any children?

J: They didn't, or they didn't survive. I didn't see a lineage there.

S: Did you see how he passed?

J: It feels intentional, that there was a hunting accident. Something along those lines, but it happened while he was supposed to be having fun. He was supposed to relax and take his mind off of something. It feels like part of his skull is shattered, that something hits his head, but I can't see what.

S: Is there anything else about his life that looked interesting?

J: It looked very sad, and very depressing, and he spent his life trying to be something that he was not. He was never good enough for what people around him wanted, and ultimately it brought relief to him to die at an early age. After that lifetime, he was relieved to go somewhere else where he could be happy with his gifts, with who he was, rather than trying to be Pharaoh-like and mighty and see something that he could not.

S: Where did he go after that life?

J: It looks like he was rested for a short amount of time before he reviewed his life because he was very eager to go through it, he was very eager to get past this life. He then takes a life as a very simple young man not far from Egypt. But he goes where he felt he was wanted and useful. He was special and people recognized him for his gifts. I see him working with natural things, like with wood, creative things. One of the gifts that he taps into is making very aesthetic things, some of them are carvings out of wood.

S: Is his soul on the Earth now, in a body?

J: In several bodies now is what I see. If I look from above, it looks like he's in several different places and in several different bodies, both male and female.

S: Did you see this information when you were working with Julie?

J: A lot of it, but not all of it.

S: Did the two of you record this information that you were getting?

J: No, we didn't collect it into anything.

CHAPTER 7: THE CHRISTMAS PARTY

As we were sifting through the memories of Christie's life, it became apparent that there had been one incident in particular that served as the catalyst to her demise, an incident at a Christmas party that ultimately led to her being committed to an insane asylum. Below are the harrowing details of the night that would change Christie's life forever.

S: Ok, let's leave that scene, and move ahead in time to where something important is happening, be there now. What do you notice?

J: It looks like it is Christmas time. I see the multicolored lights all over and I feel very apprehensive that I have to go to a work party for the holidays.

S: Could you describe yourself?

J: I have on a burgundy-colored dress that is made out of… looks like a corduroy material and it's right above my knees. It's maybe a little shorter than it should have been, and it feels like I made this dress. But it was the only red/burgundy outfit that I owned. It was the only thing that I had with the colors that I thought were of the holiday season. I don't think I have a lot of money or resources. I feel very dependent on everything I can get, use, and reuse, and I feel very self-conscious in this dress because I didn't have enough material to make it longer!

S: You feel self-conscious?

J: Yes, very, and I feel like I'm constantly looking around, hoping that I'm not sending the wrong message out. Because it's just a matter of poverty rather than wanting to attract people with what I'm wearing. And I know it will be taken the wrong way because the women that I'm going to see at this party are very judgmental.

S: Tell me about that.

J: I work with these women at this news station up in this building and they are all very exclusionary. They have their own clique within themselves. They are not even friends with one another really, but they are just extra combative when it comes to me. There is a strong jealousy factor there towards me from many of them.

S: How does that make you feel?

J: It's horrible. It isn't what I was looking for. I just wanted to have a good job where I made a good salary and where I was taken seriously by people, but I feel that I can't get to that point, that I can't sustain myself here. There are too many people who are working against me for no other reason than how I look.

S: *Tell me about how you look?*

J: I am stunning in many ways. Stunning in the way where I refuse to accept it or acknowledge it. I'm just a very beautiful looking person with a thin and shapely body. I'm about five foot eight I would say, and I just look "all American" with the blond hair and blue eyes. I look like a person that people would look at and say, "I would like to look like that, I wish I had been born that way," but it was not that way for me. It was terrible, and a curse. I could never find people to befriend me. I also could never find men who would be truthful and honest with me. I could never make friends with women, and I felt that people constantly leered at me. I always felt that they were looking for ways to corner me, or to touch me, or to do things to me that they felt they wanted to do without my permission. And this was a constant thing. I was never safe or given rest from it.

S: *Did you enjoy being beautiful in any way, or no?*

J: No, there was no enjoyment in it because I could not feel good about myself when it created such a rift with everyone around me. And I even felt that my mother saw me as competition, especially as I grew up. She felt that she needed to get rid of me in order for her husband, or other men to keep looking at her when we walked around together. At first my mother had used me to get this type of attention and to bring it to her, but now that I was older, she didn't want it anymore, and it drove a wedge between us as well.

S: *Tell me more about the Christmas party. What happens?*

J: I didn't want to go! I knew something would go wrong there. I remember that it was snowing outside, and I was miserably cold. I was cold because my jacket did not go much further down my body than my dress did. But I knew I needed to be dressed in a certain way, so I wore this anyway, even though I was freezing. I also thought I would bring some cookies with me that I made. They were on a plate and the plate had brown paper wrapped all around it, and when I got outside the ice was so slippery that I fell and dropped them. I was devastated because I was already nervous about going and now, I really didn't want to go to the party without anything to contribute. I thought that going empty handed would make a bad impression, but I knew that because it was a work party that I had to go anyway.

S: *Tell me more.*

J: When I showed up, no one wanted to talk to me as I had feared. I had gone over to certain people to speak to them and to try to be social, but they wouldn't really interact with me. Some of them would say a few words and then go to speak to other people. I don't know what is wrong with me, why this is happening, why I can't communicate or connect with people here… or anywhere. I feel so isolated. I just constantly want to have this human interaction, but the way I look puts me in a certain position where no one wants to get to know me. They just want to either possess me or hate me.

S: What happens next?

J: I'm given a drink and I feel a little tipsy, which makes me also feel more open with people. And I start talking to one woman in particular who doesn't quickly get up to go. She has bright auburn/red hair, almost like a bright but dark auburn. Does that make sense? She's an older woman, and she's talks to me. I've had a few drinks at this point, and I start to tell her a little about my experiences in understanding past lives. I tell her some other things that I thought were interesting about what I had begun to understand through staring at a candle with the help of a woman Julie. And I tell her about the candle because there is a candle in front of us on a little table that they have set up for the party.

S: Tell me more.

J: The table is small and round and comes up to about my chest. And I can look into that candle as I talk to her. And I start to see things about her in this candle as we're talking. And then she begins to talk, and I get this feeling that I shouldn't talk to her anymore, I shouldn't continue.

S: You have that feeling?

J: Yes, but I've had a few drinks and I think that this feeling might just be me trying to hide and keep everything to myself. I've been told that I need to start getting out and getting out of my head more.

S: What happens next?

J: She begins to call people over to listen to my story, and she acts like it's fascinating. And then when these people start listening to me, they all begin to act like it's fascinating as well. They act like I've uncovered this massive story, like this is something they've all been interested in. I feel finally like these people are about to accept me! Like they are about to let me be a part of this group and work environment. And then when I finish talking, they completely humiliate me. They talk about how crazy I am, and what a good story it was that I've created. Someone asks me if I'm taking medication. My boss has overheard everything, and he asks me to stay behind after the party has ended, stay behind after everyone leaves.

S: Your boss asked you to stay after the party?

J: I thought I was going to be fired. I thought he was going to tell me that I couldn't talk about that stuff anymore, but he pretended that he was interested in it. He told me that he wanted me to stay behind to talk about it more. He gave me another drink and I told him more about it. When I started talking, he started to get disgusting with me. He starts touching me by massaging my shoulders and playing with my hair from behind me. Then as he does this, he then goes in and kisses my neck... and I froze...I froze. I didn't know what to do. I tried moving away from him and I tried to move out of the room. I was just so disgusted with it all. I didn't know what to do.

S: Tell me more. What happens next?

J: I push myself away from him, almost like I was frozen at first and then suddenly reacting with a jolt. As I react, he pushes me up against this window. I'm so afraid, and I see the snow is just swirling all around outside. I know it will be freezing when I run out of there. And I'm able to duck underneath him and get out. I start running down the flights of stairs, and as I do, I fall down one of them and I lose my shoes and sprained my ankle, but I managed to keep going.

S: Tell me more.

J: When I get to the subway, I'm relieved that it's warmer there, but my feet are so cold that they are absolutely freezing. There's no one down here in this subway tonight, it's completely empty. I just feel so disgusted with myself! I feel so mad at myself that I shared that information with those people. How could I have been so stupid! I don't know how I will ever get over this terrible feeling of shame, anger, and embarrassment. And I look at the trains coming, and I think about just jumping in front of one of the trains but somehow, I manage to talk myself out of it.

S: What information did you tell those people at the party?

J: I told them all that there was a land that I was a Queen of, and that this land was destroyed by a wave that stood taller than anything I had ever seen before. I told them how this wave destroyed my land and my people, and it took my family away from me. I told them how I was taken to another place, another island where people had technology more advanced than us. I told them about the experiments and how I was experimented on. I told them that I saw other beings who help us from the stars. And I explained some of these things to them. They acted like it was so interesting, they acted like it was something amazing that I had uncovered. But it was just a big joke for them!

S: What happened after you got to the subway?

J: I take the subway back to where I live. I'm still living with my friend's mom and her children. When I see her, I try to talk to her because I'm so upset and desperately want to feel better. And she just tells me that I need to go to bed and to just sleep it off. She says that I'd had too many drinks and that I was too upset and that I should just go to sleep. But I was so desperate to tell someone! My friend's mother was just too tired to talk to me. She had had a long day and it just wasn't the right timing.

S: So, what did you do?

J: I barely slept, but when I woke up the next morning, I still didn't know what to do. I was hoping, and thought that if I just went to work, I could pretend that none of what happened last night had actually happened. Maybe it didn't, I tried to convince myself. Maybe I had just drunk too much and thought that I had said these things when I actually didn't. This is what I tried to tell myself. Also, maybe all of the people who had listened to my stories had drunk a lot as well, and maybe they wouldn't really remember what I had talked about. But when I walked into work, trying to pretend that nothing had happened, I realized that I had made a huge mistake. My heart sank, and the shame hit me like a ton of bricks in my stomach, as I could see a strange look on all of my co-worker's faces as I walked through that door.

S: Tell me more.

J: It felt like I was just frozen in the middle of the entry way when I walked in. I couldn't even move. Everyone was just looking at me. They were all staring at me. They looked amazed that I was even there! They looked like they couldn't believe that I would come back after what happened the night before. Then my boss asked me to come to his office again and I was terrified. I was terrified to be around him after what he had tried to do to me the night before! He asked me what I remembered from last night. And instead of talking about all of the pervy things that he was trying to do to me, he starts talking about how crazy I am, and how I can't work there anymore, and that I make everyone uncomfortable. And then he says that this isn't going to work out. We get into an argument after that, and he has security take me out. I'm hysterical too and they call an ambulance and take me away.

S: Why do you become hysterical during the argument?

J: I kept trying to point out to him that what I had experienced during my sessions with Julie was something that I had experienced, and just something to take into consideration, and not something I was trying to change about their world. And that the real problem I was having was the fact that he had tried to make a move on me last night, and I wasn't comfortable with that. Then he acted like that never happened, that he would never touch me inappropriately, that I had made that up and that I was just crazy! He said that I was absolutely crazy! It looked like he had planned this whole thing through the night. It appeared that he had planned that if I did come back in to work and tried to talk to anyone about what had happened, and the inappropriate behavior that he displayed last night, that he was basically ready to have me sent away to a mental hospital for an evaluation…which seems like it was very easy for him to coordinate.

S: Oh. Tell me about that.

J: It seems like it was easy and convincible that a woman speaking about anything like what I was speaking about at the party would have to be crazy, and people would be more than willing to take you into a mental facility for an observation, a two-week observation.

CHAPTER 8: MEMORIES OF AN EXTRA-TERRESTRIAL LIFETIME

As I uncovered more about what happened after the Christmas party that led to the mental institution, I realized that Jen had many more memories of her life as an extra-terrestrial.

S: What happened when you got to the mental institution?

J: They said I was suffering from a very common issue called female hysteria, and that I needed time away, and that I was to stay in this building. They said many women experience this issue because of their hormones. They said that they would take care of me, and they claimed that they would give me the right medications and help me get back on my feet again. As soon as I arrived it was obvious that they were simply just putting on a show and pretending that they were there to help me. In actuality, they were not interested in helping me at all!

S: What do you mean?

J: They really wanted to make money off of me by keeping me there, and they were not looking to help me at all. And they are not listening or have any interest in listening to me at all! They are constantly telling me that anything I say is a figment of my imagination and that it's very common for women to overindulge in their imagination, and if I keep taking the medication, and doing the scheduled things that I'm supposed to do, that I will get better. They have us do these stupid things that are supposed to help us relax.

S: What kinds of things?

J: It's not meditation, it looks like breathing exercises. We have to breathe in and out for long periods of time, which just seems so ridiculous. They keep telling me that if I do this then I won't have those memories anymore. They call them false memories, that's the label they give them. They say that I have just become hysterical, and it is probably a result of my hormones, and they keep telling me that it is a common thing that happens to some women!

S: How does this make you feel?

J: Soo frustrated because I know that hysteria is not what this is! My memories of my life in Lemuria and Atlantis are something I have come to understand, and they are meaningful. They refuse to see it this way, they only see me as something to make money off of. They don't even see me as a person.

S: What happens next?

J: There's a psychiatrist that I see every day. He's a shorter man with a full set of hair that he's cut short. I can tell that he's preoccupied with other things going on in his life, and he's not really there to help anyone, but just to collect his salary and go home. It seems obvious to me that he has issues at home, and he just brushes me off whenever I try to talk to him. He's so preoccupied, I think his wife is having an affair and he is always thinking about his life outside of this hospital. He doesn't even listen to what I'm saying. He treats me just like another one of his patients who's had a breakdown, or schizophrenia.

S: Tell me more.

J: No one listens to me. After a certain amount of time, they allow me to make phone calls and I call my mom and she won't help me.

S: What does she say?

J: She says she can't do anything to help me, that this is where I have brought myself and that I have to be the one to get myself out of it. Then I called the mother of my friend, where I was staying, and she is too overwhelmed with her own children to help me through this. Then I called Julie. She tries to tell me that it is up to me to get myself out of there. That there is nothing that she can do for me at this point, that this is not what she intended for me, and she is sorry, but there is nothing she can do on her end to get me out of this place. I feel that I'm in Brooklyn NY, that I'm in a very big medical facility there.

S: Where do you feel that you are?

J: I feel that I'm definitely not in Manhattan, that I'm on the other side of the water there and that's where they have taken me.

S: Are there any windows in this place?

J: Yes, there's a small window in the common room. There's a wired sheet of metal that goes through it to stop people from breaking it, or from jumping out of the window.

S: Can you see anything through the window? Can you see what it looks like outside?

J: Through the window I can see a little bit of the water. I can sit there and look at it, and I actually do this a lot, because I feel that the ability to sit there and look at this little bit of water is the only thing that I have left. I feel that I spend most of the time that I'm given in this communal room, looking out this window.

S: What do you do there?

J: I just keep to myself and look out this window. I feel that after a while I begin to rock back in forth for some reason.

S: *Why do you do that?*

J: It just begins after a while because of all the rage inside of me. The rage is so strong and the only thing I can do is rock back and forth because nobody will listen, nobody cares. And I'm just going to die here. I'm just going to die inside this place. Eventually someone is just going to do something to me and either I'm going to kill them, or I'm going to kill myself. All I can think of is that I have to get out of there.

S: *Ok, let's leave that scene and move ahead in time, what happens next?*

J: They start to perform shock treatments on me.

S: *Why?*

J: That is just what they do, they don't care at all about me.

S: *What is that like? You can see this as an observer, you don't have to feel this memory.*

J: The tables were very cold and very narrow, and they had these bars that would come down by my arms that they would strap my arms to. The leather straps were very thick and very disgusting. They felt like they were soaked with people's sweat and blood, and just all kinds of disgusting things within it. And on top of the leather strap there was a metal clasp on it that was very big, like a locking mechanism, and it was very heavy. It just felt so dehumanizing to be in this room, to be strapped to this device. There was a nurse in there as well.

S: *What was she like?*

J: She wears a mask on her face to protect her from people spitting on her. The patients liked to spit on her during this. Sometimes voluntary, sometimes involuntarily. But during these treatments I began to remember more about my other lifetimes.

S: *Tell me more, what would you remember?*

J: The shock treatments were extremely painful, but within the pain itself it would allow me to see more within myself, and I could see more about my life as the commander on a different planet.

S: *Could you tell me more about that life?*

J: I grew up differently than what we would experience as young children on Earth. In this world where I lived as an extra-terrestrial, a person was created. You are designed, created, and then you are placed within families who will raise you as theirs.

S: Who designs each person?

J: We do. It was a common thing that is done by our people. It was almost like an elite designer baby system that had allowed us to create better people. It allowed us to further our technology and our advancements because of it, and it had been going on for quite some time before me. Many, many generations had come through this system, more than I could begin to count.

S: What was the process like?

J: They incubated you in what was like an artificial womb because they could not procreate at this stage of our evolution, and there was a scientific way to do it rather than the natural way. They could no longer continue to procreate in the natural way because they had evolved past that ability, and we also couldn't gestate our own children any longer.

S: Were there natural births before this?

J: Yes, a long time ago, but we had evolved out of this.

S: Why?

J: We had hit a certain point where we were able to manipulate the genetic codes that were within us and we were able to change these codes in ways that changed the minds of our people. It wasn't as physical as it was mental. It allowed for more advancement, for people to think differently, and we stopped having as many unproductive attachments because of this manipulation.

S: What was your life like growing up on this planet?

J: From a very early age I was reared towards my career in the space exploration program. I was tested as a child, and this was what I showed the greatest natural aptitude towards. However, I was designed for this as well. My genetics were designed to have this type of aptitude, and I progressed on schedule, and I was ushered into this program of exploration. It was lonely growing up on this planet though. There was a mother and father figure, but they were not present very much after I finished my education.

S: What was your relationship like with your parents?

J: It was very congenial. It was not a deep and loving relationship, but rather a pre-agreed upon relationship that we both understood and needed to fulfill. We did not create a deep attachment to each other's souls within this agreement. Don't get me wrong they were adequate care givers, but on the planet where I grew up there was a different type of caring and nurturing, which is much colder in practice than what we understand as nurturing on the Earth planet. But I grew up on this planet the way I was supposed to, and my parents fulfilled their jobs. This was just how we functioned.

S: What was your father like?

J: I remember my father telling me about the Red and the Blue planets. I remember looking at them at night and watching them. They were close to our planet, and you could see them just like you can see the moon from Earth.

S: *Could you tell me more about these planets that you could see from yours?*

J: The Red and the Blue planet were within our galaxy. The blue one was to the left and the red one was located a little bit further down and to the right. I remember my father telling me about the people that worked on the red planet who were mining the energy. The red one had a lot of mining on it.

S: *What type of mining?*

J: They were always looking for, and mining, a type of energy out of the planet. It was something like oil, a petroleum, although it was not in a liquid form. It was more of a fluid energy form, but it functioned like gasoline, and it powered our devices.

S: *What type of devices do you have?*

J: Devices that were similar to a car that could float and propel you forward in very fast movements. It was based on propulsion, and it could move you up and outwards.

S: *How does this work?*

J: The energy this used was dark in color and worked with a device that was in the ship. It looked like kinetic energy was harnessed within a glass tube and it worked similar to the way that opposite ends of a magnet work. And this energy could propel our devices forward and upwards. This is the energy that they mine and that they put into these vehicles, these crafts.

S: *Who mines this?*

J: Another race of beings that are much smaller than us. They are not from our planet; they are just somehow stuck here.

S: *Tell me more.*

J: These small beings seem very depressed; they each die eventually from the effects of mining this energy, but they are aware of this as they do so.

S: *Do you get a sense of where they are from? Why are they there?*

J: It was part of the ancient history of our planet. They were seeking shelter and safety with us, but they did not do well on our planet. They were taken to the red planet, and they weren't forced to be there or to do this work, they just found purpose in it. They are stuck there because they have nowhere else to go. I remember my father would talk about these people and tell me how we all have our role to fulfill within this society. That we all have goals and accomplishments, but we all work towards a common goal.

S: What was this common goal?

J: It looks like it was the advancement, of moving away from this planet and going into the unknown, going to the colonies we had created on other planets. This was towards the end of our planet's life cycle. We needed to learn to leave and go to the next.

S: Why was it the end of your planet's life cycle?

J: The planet was towards the end of its life, and it had done its job, and it was tired and was dying. Like a beautiful tree trunk that you find in the woods. It is still something and still beautiful, but it is dead inside and has very little life left to give. It is just the natural progression of how planets are supposed to go.

S: When you left your planet to go on the exploration to Earth, could you tell me more about that?

J: I was so excited to go to Earth! My whole life felt like it had culminated to that point. I felt everything was beginning with that journey, that this was something new to experience, something that was beyond what I had learned and known in my training. I had never left the realm of my planet, or the red or the blue planet before. I had never gone through the wormhole or gone through the passageway to Earth. I had dreamt of this as a younger version of myself.

S: Could you tell me more about your planet?

J: It was more like Earth in its history, but it also started to look more like Mars as it gets closer to the end. Towards the end it started to have a very rough terrain, and it started to become desolate, it almost looks like an orange that starts to turn grey.

S: Could you tell me more about what your planet used to look like?

J: It had a similar structure to Earth. There was oxygen in its atmosphere that we breathe, and there was also water and land. But there were things that were different such as the placement of the land masses on our planet.

S: How were they different?

J: On my planet there was more of a Pangea than on Earth where the land masses are spread out. On my planet the water decreased eventually. The water started to evaporate, dry up as our planet was dying. That wasn't the cause of its destruction, just a byproduct of it.

S: When you left on your exploration to Earth had the water already dried up?

J: I am seeing my planet at different points in its history right now as I remember this information coming to me during the shock treatments that they performed. I saw my planet and how it began, all the way up to when it became desolate nothingness. But there is still, within the grey nothingness, **these towers with these spires on my planet. They are still there even now. The planet that I lived on has these towers that stick up and they look like they are made of copper, and they make very strange angles that go up into the sky that look somewhat like a radio antenna that's sending out information.**

S: What are they used for? Why are they still there?

J: It is something that was built before this planet was uninhabitable and it was left as a record of our existence there. With the right technology you could tap into this device, and you could pull out the full history of this planet.

S: What type of technology would someone need to use to access this information?

J: For some, just a passageway through the mind would take you there. For others who would come across it and visit, they would need to have another type of metal that needs to touch the spires to unleash this information and unfurl this history. This metal looks like a circle touching another circle, turning, and pushing in, and a blue light emanating from it.

S: What kind of history would you see if you were to look at these records?

J: It is very similar to our history on Earth with our developments! But for us on this other planet that I'm remembering, evolution went a lot faster. We did not have a long process; things went faster in our development. We were also brought to this planet too, just like we were brought to Earth. This planet that I'm seeing was not the beginning. It was just another steppingstone to where we are going.

S: Where are we going exactly?

J: We are going everywhere and nowhere all at once. It is not a physical place that we are going to. In this evolution, changing of planets, traveling through these worm holes we change. **How we changed is what is important in all of this.**

S: How have we changed since the beginning?

J: For us on Earth now we have become way more involved in our physical bodies. We have created all kinds of rules about them that truly don't exist. For instance, we believe that we have physical limitations, but really, we have just created that within our own minds. They are completely just things we have created. Some of the changes are not always good and, in some ways, we have fallen behind.

S: Tell me more about that.

J: Earth is not the only planet that has been seeded, there are many others out there and they are not always just like us. They evolve differently and aren't as harsh on themselves or as difficult. There is a certain air of darkness that we have brought upon ourselves in our evolution here. And that is one of the ways we have changed. We are less optimistic on a universal level.

S: Why was that darkness around us?

J: There was a fear virus that followed us to this planet, that attached itself to one of our ships and followed us through the worm hole. It has tarred this experiment and infected us.

S: Tell me more.

J: To release this fear one needs to not be afraid of it, to allow fear to disappear. It isn't something someone can do consciously on their own. There is planning behind this.

S: Tell me more.

J: Many have decided in this lifetime that they will cast off this fear and there are many predestined plans that have been organized. There have been many plans or situations organized and set that are creating all these scenarios allowing this to happen. It can't be forced, and everyone will have their turn to release their fear.

S: When you left your planet and went on your mission to Earth, did you have any expectations?

J: My expectations were that my ship would arrive undamaged, that I would be in charge, and that my crew would not be challenging in the ways that they were. I expected this to go smoothly, and I expected to go back to my planet with the human/ hybrid children we were looking to create. I expected to succeed in this experiment and to show proof that we can continue this experiment on Earth. We couldn't live on Earth the way we were because our skin was too light, the UV rays would damage us too quickly, and we needed to breed with the humans to create a hybrid being who could live and thrive. We needed this to work in order to eventually inhabit these human bodies.

S: What happened?

J: There were problems on the ship. I heard an alarm that alerted me that the breathing mechanisms were failing and that we would have to crash land our ship on Earth quickly. That was how they purposely set this crash up, because we can't breathe in the atmosphere up above Earth without these mechanisms. We could however breathe on Earth; we do have the same ability to breathe oxygen, and that was another reason why we came here to seed Earth.

S: Were you misled, since your ship crashed?

J: I believe I was misled by my superiors in believing that I would be able to help create this new world. I knew others would also be going to Earth and would be doing the same thing and would also be going with their ships and creating these communities as well. But I felt our mission was going to be special. I felt that we were going to create something truly unbelievable and that we would truly succeed in this before any of the others did. I felt that we were going to be the pilot program, the first, best, and the most successful. And when I look back, I realize that we were in many ways. But nothing truly does last forever.

S: Was there a purpose for you to have crashed in the place that you did?

J: Yes. It was to get close to the grouping of people that we knew were growing in numbers and we were supposed to find them. The crash itself looks as if our superiors had been maneuvering this for us to see how things would go if we did not have our equipment. But we did not know this beforehand. They wanted to see how we would react. And the intentional crash was so that we may never return. This was a one-way mission.

S: Tell me more about that.

J: Our ships were rigged and made to crash. Our superiors weren't looking to kill any of us but that did take place, and some of our crew did perish. That was negligence of our superiors. We could have prepared better if they had given us this understanding that this was going to happen. I was in charge of these people and to allow them to die on my watch was something that I didn't feel I could process. (Jen started to cry) I wish I had understood during that lifetime that it wasn't my fault; it wasn't me who had caused that crash. I wish I had known that what I believed to have been the failure of our experiment was truly not my fault and I wish I had seen that it wasn't a failure after all. But it was only something I learned after I left that life.

S: When your crew members who passed during the crash of your ship left their bodies, were they given that knowledge?

J: I see that it was revealed to them in their life review. They understood that this was part of their life contract that they needed to fulfill by having these traumatic deaths after a great adventure. It was part of their itinerary of the things that they wanted to accomplish during that life.

S: Are life contracts the same on your planet and this planet?

J: They are the same. It doesn't matter where our physical bodies are. It is in the same in-between that we all go to, and all create these contracts.

S: What about the other ships that crashed?

J: It looks like they were all meant to crash as well. They were all aiming towards where there had been sprinklings of the DNA of the early humans we had been creating. There had been a lot of visitations observing the growth of these specimens. Time was very different on Earth than it was on the home planet.

S: Tell me more.

J: We could be gone for a certain amount of time but only feel like a couple of years had passed on our planet, while for Earth it may be ten thousand years. And in this way, we were able to watch very quickly the evolution of Earth, from basic amoebas to humans take place.

S: *Were the other crashes a result of them being misled as well?*

J: There were no pilots who knew in advance that they were going to crash their ships, but it also looks like some who were not supposed to crash did so in an odd accident where the ship had a malfunction when it entered Earth's atmosphere. There were intentional ones, and a few that crashed unintentionally. They wanted to see what would happen in all these different communities with this type of technology or without this type of technology. The purpose was to see what worked best in moving forward as we colonized this planet. What environments would work best? What foods would work best? What technologies? What should we create with our technologies for these humans? Would it make them smarter? Would it make them greedy? Would it make them useless? All the variants were to see all of the different potentials for the future of this planet.

S: *Tell me more.*

J: We knew that Earth was something that we could begin to colonize. Colonizing Earth meant that we would be able to continue our kind. We knew that this was connected to something much bigger than us in that we knew that we were meant to find this planet. This is like what finding the New World is for those of us on this Earth. It is something that has been created by us, for us, as a way for us all to continue this experiment. The New World is next in line in this long continuum of planets we have lived on.

S: *What do you mean by the New World?*

J: *We are always looking for new planets to seed because there always needs to be a backup planet in case of the unthinkable, and there is another Earth we are seeding right now that you would call the New World.*

S: *How does the Earth that we are living on now look? Does it look like it will die anytime soon?*

J: It does not. It is blue, green, and white and very healthy right now. Even though parts of this Earth are sick, it is still not at its halfway mark.

S: *Why are parts of it sick?*

J: This Earth has become overpopulated, and it was not meant for this many people. This will change over the next twenty years and change the ways we are living. More people will move to rural areas and have fewer children.

S: *Any other changes you notice in the next twenty years?*

J: There are too many variables in the future potentials, but it looks very promising even though there are potentials for natural disasters that may cause a shift. There will also be many changes in the technology that will be available to us on this Earth, especially in the way we travel through water. The water will clean itself out. We will find a way to collect and use garbage found in the water and use it to our benefit, and our planet Earth will continue.

CHAPTER 9: MORE MEMORIES UNCOVERED IN A MENTAL HOSPITAL

Jen's memories of the mental hospital can only be described as horrific and disturbing. As Jen and I uncovered these memories, I was appalled at how recently they occurred. I was reminded of my own experience when I, too, saw firsthand this unfortunate truth, in my young twenties as a Psychology student. I had every intention of continuing my studies with graduate school when I took an internship as a counselor in a halfway house for mentally ill residents. As I know now there are no coincidences, my experience there truly shined a light on our extremely limited ability as a culture to help mentally ill people. After this experience, I chose not to pursue a career in psychology, unsettled by the impression that patients were actually exploited by the pharmaceutical industry rather than nurtured by it. My experience, and the one recalled by Jen shines a harrowing light on the dysfunction of our conventional healthcare.

S: How long had you been in the mental institution before they started to do these shock treatments to you?

J: I was only there three to four days before they started doing this to me. I don't feel like they even really spoke to me before they gave me the shock treatments. Almost like that was their initial protocol and the chosen thing to do instead of actually finding out what the issue I had was. Maybe they hoped that perhaps the shock treatments would sedate me enough that they wouldn't have to deal with me, and I would stop acting crazy. No one there was there to help me get better, or to help me leave this place. I was there to be kept there. I was not there to be helped.

S: What about the other people in there? Do you get a sense if anyone else there was at all like you? Not actually mentally debilitated?

J: Yes, there were others there like me! I can't remember them all that clearly right now, but there was one girl in particular that I clearly remember. She was a little bit younger than me, and she had short hair with tight curls that were brushed out a bit to make her hair look a bit poufy and short.

S: Did you ever talk to her or get a sense as to why she was there?

J: She was like me. I remember that we had an understanding that we were there for the same reason. We were not crazy, but we could not voice this to people because no one cared or even wanted to listen. But she had been there longer than me and she wasn't there to make a friend at first. She knew what happened to everyone once they came in. No one ever left. Once you were in there it was rare if anyone ever left the place. Most people only left if they left in a body bag. This girl told me all about the different people.

S: What did she tell you?

J: She told me about how some of the residents there would use different objects, like sharp edges of tables or anything that they would find to try to cut their wrists open with it. She told me that people would look for anything sharp, anything that they could find to do this with, anything that they could break apart. There were no mirrors there for this reason. There was no cutlery even. There was nothing that you could obviously do this with so some people would even just try to use their teeth and rip away at themselves. And then, when they would do this, they would have to then be restrained. But they would always keep trying to do these things. Sometimes suddenly out of nowhere someone would be next to you and would just start biting themselves, biting at their wrists. And the staff would just come running over and throw them to the floor and throw their hands down. And their feet would kick all over the place. At first, I used to just back away from it, but as I spent more and more time there I didn't back away. I think I was just waiting for one of them to just knock me out. I just wanted to die as well. I just wanted to get out of there so badly. I just wanted to be taken away.

S: Did you try to reach out to Julie and your friend's mom again?

J: No. They only allowed me to make a few phone calls when I first got there after I demanded that I needed to call someone, that I had to call my mother. They allowed me to do it only once. I called my mother and I called Julie and they both abandoned me.

S: What did your mother say?

J: My mother said that it was not possible for her to help me. She was involved with someone who wouldn't allow her to have a life outside of him. She was with another controlling man. She was in the same situation again where she was just pulling away from me. She won't help me! I'm only just an accessory to her. I'm there to be used, but when I need help, she feels no obligation to be a mother, and it becomes very clear to me when I hang up with her, that that's the last time that I'm ever going to talk to her again.

S: What about Julie? What did she say when you called her?

J: Her reaction was much more difficult to manage than my mother's reaction was, even though I had only known Julie for such a short period of time. I felt that I had trusted her and that she would be there to guide me, but it was superficial. She was not experienced enough to handle the situation that I was in. She acted very overwhelmed when I told her where I was. And instead of looking to back me up and help me get out of here by coming to this facility and explaining to these people that I'm not crazy, that this has been a misunderstanding, she instead told me that I have just gotten myself too far into something, and she doesn't want to deal with it.

S: How does that make you feel?

J: It feels worse than my mother abandoning me. With Julie I felt like we were uncovering all of this knowledge together, and it feels like a slap in the face that she won't help me. It feels like the crushing off of that world when I finished that phone call. And when that call ends, I know it is the last time I'm going to speak to Julie as well.

S: Could she have helped you if she had gone to your facility and claimed that you weren't crazy?

J: When I look at it from this perspective, I see that there could've been some intervention if someone, anyone, had come to my aid. If someone had spoken in my defense or if someone besides my boss had filled out a report or spoken to any of the employees there, then my stay would've been much shorter, and I could've restarted my life in a different manner. But I was not given that chance and I was not able to convince anyone there that I was sane. It was of no benefit to anyone to prove that I was sane. There was no incentive for anyone to help me, and especially when it came to anyone in the facility. It was obvious that they were not there to listen or to help me; they were there to make sure that I was there and that was it.

S: Tell me more about what it was like there in that facility, that mental hospital? What else do you remember?

J: The screaming was terrible! You could hear it all over this place. And it wasn't just one kind of screaming. There were these horrible repetitive shrieks over and over and over again in so many different tones, coming from so many different places, especially at night. The night was the worst. There was no way anyone there slept, and I think that also contributed to many of us looking like we were insane. The dark circles under all of our eyes were because there was no way you could sleep there. The screaming was not just at night, but at all hours during the day as well. There was one person that I remember clearly, and all he did was just hit his head against the wall, all day long. Sometimes the people that worked there just didn't care, they would just let him hit his head against the wall until he knocked himself out, and when he did you could hear the thud. It was so disgusting. I can still hear it. It was just sickening; you were just waiting for that crack sound when he hit the ground. And that was usually when somebody else would start up and make some other disgusting sounds and some people would even make sounds like an animal or a whale. The nighttime was just a chorus of absolute craziness. Every night… every night.

S: Did anyone watch over you at night? Any guards?

J: The guards were horrible people. The guards were mostly there to either torture people, to turn a blind eye and collect a paycheck, or to take advantage of people sexually.

S: Tell me more about that.

J: There was one guard in particular who took advantage of me, and I was often incapacitated for it.

S: How were you incapacitated?

J: They would tie you to the beds at night and the guards could take advantage of you by putting you in a special area, solitary confinement area, and it was very easy for them to do. They would make a false claim that you were having an unstable… I remember there was a code for it even. They would call it in, and it was just absolute B.S. It was never really because they were actually worried about someone or that the person was actually unstable. It was a way for the guards to take advantage of the people they were attracted to, and these people that they were attracted to were constantly being put into these solitary confinement cells.

S: *What would happen when they would put you in there?*

J: They would put you in there and then they would strap you to the bed and both of your arms would be strapped in with these leather straps, and I remember that the bed frames were cold and metal. And that's where you were supposed to stay. And these disgusting guards could do whatever they wanted to you. I remember one night I was put in there and I was crying so hard that I could barely feel my chest. It was hurting from all the crying, and I could feel my eyes becoming swollen and incredibly painful. The salt of my tears burned the skin around my eyes because I couldn't wipe the tears away while they had both of my arms strapped to the bed. And I kept crying and thinking that I just needed to get out of there. I didn't want to die in that horrible place!

S: *What kind of things would they do to you?*

J: They were disgusting, and they could do anything that they wanted to you. Sometimes they would take items and laugh as they stuck them inside of you. Sometimes they would just full on rape people. These special rooms, the solitary confinement cells were just rooms of horror. The guards were absolutely disgusting. This place where this hospital was is still haunted. I can sense this deeply as I see it from this perspective. The screaming is very much still there. It's an energy that stays and it echoes throughout this place. It is in the brick, in the mold that holds it together.

S: *Tell me more about how you spent your days there? Is there anything else that you notice that seems important?*

J: I remember that when I would receive the shock treatments that they would also give me some sort of a relief, and I would actually look forward to this torture as a way to escape my reality and the horror around me. At first, I would feel this shooting pain going through my body. It would go from my head all the way down my body like it was going into my heart, but then it would shoot out to my legs, toes and my fingers and I couldn't breathe. I couldn't move. I would be in so much pain. The extreme pain was burning, cold, and everything all at once. And the pain would hit a point where right before I blacked out I could, all of a sudden, feel this connection, this ability to go beyond myself.

S: *Tell me more about that.*

J: It was my release; it allowed me to escape from this torture that I found myself in. I felt like I was connecting with something beyond myself while the electricity continued to go through my body.

S: *Do you get a sense as to what you were connecting to?*

J: I could connect back to the beginning of Earth.

S: *What did you notice when you connected back to the beginning of Earth?*

J: I could see these happy people. I could see them experimenting and I could see these facilities where they were learning and growing, and this was a relaxed and joyous environment. My mind took me to this place, and it allowed me to escape there, before I blacked out. And once I would black out, I felt like I could go anywhere. I was unstoppable. I no longer needed any guidance. It was just a rogue mission now to get away from this situation that was around me, and to just go somewhere else.

S: *Where would you go?*

J: Somewhere within myself where I would often see the Sphinx, when it still had the jungle cat façade.

S: Tell me more. Why did you see the Sphinx?

J: This was a symbol for me to see to remind me of better times, and through almost like passageways within the Sphinx, I was brought to wherever I needed to go that brought me to a place of comfort and joy, almost like a special place if that makes sense.

S: *Yes. Tell me more about it. What was this special place like?*

J: It wasn't just this place. It looks like there have been special places that I have seen like this before in many existences. But for me remembering the beginning of our experiences on Earth was such a unique time in an existence where one's life was less complicated. And while there is much less learned and much less gained, there is a special kind of comfort that comes from it that allows you to make it through some of the harder times. And the shock treatments would bring me to some of these places.

S: *Could you tell me more about the beginning of time? You saw people experimenting? Could you tell me more?*

J: It feels more like the beginning of Earth and not the beginning of time. The time aspect is not relevant.

S: *What was the beginning of Earth like?*

J: It looks like a massive explosion and things flowing through the air accumulating together and spinning together very fast. There was so much interaction and movement, way more than what we experience today on this Earth. There were so many changes in color, changes in gasses, I feel so many changes on it for a long time. And there was a constant addition and growing to the Earth, until the point comes when it is originally colonized.

S: *How was this formed? Who made the Earth exactly?*

J: The Universe has the ability to just create many of these planets and things do begin in some ways to unfold, and over time in some areas, habitable planets will emerge. They are rare and infrequent, but they are there. And when the conditions are right and the instrumentation is right, and the interaction is right, then people from the right places will come across these habitable planets and will seed them. They begin to lace the environment with genetic improvements that will benefit them. And they begin to slowly change these environments over time to allow natural evolution to occur after this instigation from an outside source.

S: Is there an intelligent source that starts this creation of the planet?

J: Yes, but it is not a person or a thing. It is a magnetic source of energy that is greater than any energy we know. This energy works in ways that pull things together. It creates and allows for things to ebb and flow. And it allows for things to make sense and for things to come together and connections to be made. And all of that is on a less than molecular level, but this magnetic energy is greater than all we know.

S: Has this source ever had a lifetime? Has it always been the way it is, or did it ever live anywhere?

J: It has, because it is the same energy that we each carry within ourselves and are made up of. The lifetimes that we have lived are all an accumulation of it on a larger all-encompassing sense. There is no difference between that energy and us when we are all combined into a greater sphere of energy.

S: So essentially, we created the Earth?

J: Yes, but we are all of it and everything within itself. Just molecularly on this very small, tiny level we separate and become different things in order to have these experiences.

S: Where was the first civilization on Earth?

J: This has happened many times before, but this most recent beginning started on the island that you would call Antarctica. There were two larger islands that were first chosen.

S: Why were they chosen?

J: They were ideal for a controlled environment that would create a more specific experiment and outcome.

S: You said that there were two islands?

J: The Earth seeding experiment started on the island of Antarctica and the island that Atlantis would eventually become. Those were the two islands. And they look like they are spaced out far enough where they look like they will have their own unique outcome, but they will also have the ability for interaction as the colonies grow. And that was the strategy within the placement of where they would begin to colonize. The placement of these two islands were specific and took into the account the understanding of the Earth's forces within itself as well as the Earth's changes that were something that would be indeterminable.

S: Why would it be indeterminable?

J: When the Earth planet was constructed and colonized, the beings doing so understood that Earth's changes would naturally need to happen. Things such as volcano eruptions and weather changes would allow for a natural flushing out and changing of the Earth. This is just the Earth's natural way of breathing and progression, and the way the Earth lives. And in order to allow the Earth to live, the colonies would have to adapt to the Earth changes.

S: So, the Earth lives through these Earth changes? Through eruptions and hurricanes?

J: Yes, those could be described as the Earth's emotions, it's life energy. It is the way it releases what it needs to, just like the way we let out our frustrations. The Earth deals with our abusive behavior in this manner, not as karma or a retribution, but as a way to release this energy that we put into it.

S: Does the Earth have just one personality or is it a combined consciousness?

J: It is a combined consciousness; we all are indefinitely a part of this larger system of particles that pull together and pull apart and become one. Our human bodies are very organic in the way that the Earth is. And it's easy to look at it as an interchanging system. This is part of what I would see when I would go through the shock therapy. I would see these places, but I would also see the people, the colonists who seeded this planet. The happiness on the colonists' and humans' faces is what I was brought there to see.

S: Tell me about that.

J: There was pure joy that radiated on their faces. These communities were made up of people and beings that were together and very happy. They were so enlightened, and they were looking to create something beautiful and different. They didn't want or expect to have the fear virus interfering with this experiment. They didn't want to have anything that would disrupt the ability for this to be a planet of good, compassion, understanding, and a planet where people and beings could live together. The intention for this planet was one where we could all prosper and grow. But that intention has been hidden from the public in order for people to feel less and do more.

S: What do you mean by that?

J: The truth of our origins has been hidden from us so that we will be more productive in a consumeristic way and so that we abide to what people would call a "normal" society and way of being. Humans are programmed to fit in and are told that fitting in is something they should strive for. But it is not. It really is just denying people the truth of our ancient heritage by considering it something that it is not.

S: What would our life be like if we accepted our ancient origins and heritage?

J: We would have a better relationship with ourselves, and we would be less detached from ourselves. We would no longer search for meaning within other people. We would have a much clearer understanding of who we are and a less difficult time understanding why we're here, what we should be doing, and what the purpose of all of this is. That is actually something that weighs on people way more than we're ever willing to admit. It keeps people acting like worker bees and part of a system that isn't serving back. There is a considerable effort to change this now.

S: Tell me more.

J: Faith must be tested to see if that is truly what you believe.

S: Why must faith be tested?

J: Because people believe things way too quickly before they ever look to see if it is true within themselves. And this is a test of that. To see for oneself if this is truly what you believe in, and if it is what you believe in, then you must live by it. It is no longer a time to sit and to half live an ideology. It is time to firm up and find what you believe in. At the end of the day that should be yourself, and nothing else.

S: Who were these smiling people that you were seeing?

J: The early colonists and many children. They were beautiful children that glowed and had these big, beautiful eyes. And when you looked at their eyes, they would sparkle. They would entrance you with their eyes. They could pull you in, and they were just lovely, so lovely to look at, and to just sit with, and to feel peace with.

S: Who were these children exactly?

J: They were hybrid children that had been created by the visitors and very early humans, very, very early humans. These children are just overjoyed to be running around and having fun with each other. The laughter is just beautiful and contagious. And everyone is just watching them and so pleased with what they have created together. They are all so happy that the children are thriving, the experiment on Earth is actually progressing; and there is a great feeling of happiness that we are seeding this new planet, this new Earth. Everything we have embarked on is all coming to fruition, and we have succeeded and look how far we have come, and we will do so much with this! We will continue our kind and we will prosper after all.

S: Do you get a sense as to why you were shown this during your shock treatments?

J: It was a calming mechanism to help me get through this, to help me move myself out of this traumatic environment and to help me get into a better state by remembering who I really was and to preserve myself before I went too far into depression and despair.

S: Why were you shown the children? Do you get a sense?

J: Their innocence was something that helps to calm, their eyes have a calming effect. It was almost like they were hypnotizing me with their eyes and the kindness and love that they had. It was very pure and very genuine. It was very strong. There was a strong connection to this love that I had never felt before in my life as Christie. This love was being given to me so freely, without consequences, without payment, without needing anything back from me.

S: *Did you have any involvement with these children? Was this a memory? Or was this just something shown to you?*

J: Looking back now I see that I was there at one point. On one of the earliest missions when we first came to Earth, I was there.

CHAPTER 10: THE LOBOTOMY

As Jen remembered more of her harrowing stay at the mental hospital, she also realized that she had uncovered even more memories after she had been lobotomized. Below are more details of Jen's memories.

S: *Ok, let's leave that scene and move ahead in time to where something else important is happening. Be there now. What is happening?*

J: (Crying) My friend! My only friend in this terrible place (sob) something happened to her!

S: *What do you mean? What happened?*

J: Something happened, I can't remember what it was, but she was yelling at the staff. I'd never even heard her yell before, but she was yelling because she didn't want to go to the solitary confinement cell anymore. I think something happened to her that she couldn't let go of. And the staff restrained her and carried her away. And when she came back, she could no longer speak. She could no longer look at me. I didn't understand what they had done to her, why she was acting this way. She couldn't even put two sentences together and she looked at me as if I was a stranger.

S: *Did you find out what happened to her?*

J: No. I just remember the anger I felt pulsing through my veins, but worst of all, the absolute despair that there was no one to help any of us in here. Because no one simply cared.

S: *Was there anything else that you noticed while living within this mental facility?*

J: I didn't see any paperwork on me. I don't think that many of the people working in this mental facility even know my name. I don't think any of them cared and I don't feel that much individual attention was given to me once I was just thrown into this place. This mental facility feels like just mass quarters. I didn't even have my own room. We were placed into big rooms where there were several beds, but many of us just slept on the floor. I feel that I slept up against a corner and I slept with my legs up to my chest, my arms wrapped around me, and my head down on my knees. And that was how I would try to sleep at night. And I would keep my legs and arms as tight around me so that I felt almost like a rock, like no one could break through me. No one could touch me. And if they did, I was ready to bounce up and just push them away, or punch, or kick them, or whatever I could, to just get them away from me.

S: Anything else about your stay there that seems important?

J: It is dirty, very dirty, there is feces and everything everywhere. People vomit all the time, and the smell is terrible. I don't think it could ever be cleaned enough so that it would ever go away. There is also quite a bit of blood on the ground and on the walls that does not get cleaned up to often. There is no fear that we would get any kind of diseases, and there was no fear of maltreatment. They don't feel that we are worth anything! They know we're not going to be leaving. The ones who do leave, leave in body bags like I said. There is no reason to clean or to do much. But there is someone who comes and mops every now and then. It's a man in a white suit, and he has two guards that go around with him and guard him as he cleans up a bit. It's never very clean, the smell is never gone, but it will remove some of the disgusting obvious stuff so that way if there ever was an inspection, it would not be a major issue.

S: Do you get a sense as to what they feed you in this place? Or how they feed you?

J: It doesn't feel like I'm fed very often or fed much. It is always like a mush, sort of akin to baby food. Everything is pureed and given to us, like a liquid diet and most of our food is given to us like that. Sometimes we get small cut up peas and carrots like the kind you get in a bag that's frozen. Sometimes we get slices of white bread, but they try not to give us too much food at once because a lot of the people there are very out of touch with what I would call reality, and they tended to try to shove the food in their mouths as fast as they could and would possibly begin choking on it. That would always lead to several of them doing this at the same time, so they try not to give us anything that we could choke on intentionally. I wasn't in here very long before I was lobotomized.

S: Why were you eventually lobotomized?

J: Because I kept trying to explain to them that I wasn't crazy. I kept pleading with them that I needed to get back to work. I kept pleading with them that I needed to make money to pay my rent so that I could have a place to live. And I pleaded with them and pestered them so much that they decided that the best way to deal with me was to lobotomize me so that they wouldn't have to deal with me anymore.

S: What was that like? What happened? You can see this as an observer with no physical discomfort whatsoever.

J: I wasn't sure what was happening at first because they didn't discuss this with me or prepare me for this at all. I thought I was just being brought in for more shock therapy, but they took me to a different room this time, and there was a doctor in there. He was wearing a green gown with a green hat on, and he had a big white mask across his face. When they brought me into this room, they quickly strapped me down again. But instead of shocking the outside, instead of hooking me up to the wires like they usually do, they pulled out a long metal tube that is connected to a long wire. The wire is connected to a machine that sits on a table and plugs into the wall. It is a surprisingly big plug that goes into it. And then they stick this thing that looks like this long metal tube all the way up my nose. As soon as they pull this long metal tube out in front of me, the fear, shock and anger of what I know they are about to do floods my body. They are going to lobotomize me! And I know my life is over.

S: *Did they give you anything before hand for the pain?*

J: No! The pain is unbearable. It just shoots through me. It is what you would feel if someone cut a piece of your brain out. I just felt this burning, like someone had poured acid down my nose. And it was just burning and burning, and I couldn't move. I couldn't do anything. I felt like I was choking on the spit that was accumulating underneath the gag that they gave me. I couldn't breathe. The tears were just coming out the sides of my eyes, I just couldn't stop crying. It just felt like so much liquid was just coming out of my face. I couldn't believe that they did this, and then suddenly something inside of me just died.

S: *Tell me more.*

J: I felt like something inside of me stopped. I can't explain what it was, but I felt a light switch just go off to my outside world. I remember the numbness. And when they took me off of all of their lobotomizing equipment and undid my restraints, I remember the feeling coming back to my fingers and toes and I remember that I was drooling. I was drooling a lot and I couldn't stop drooling. I also had another problem after this procedure where I couldn't raise my eyes up to look at people anymore. I couldn't string a sentence together. I just couldn't function outwardly, but inside my brain still worked.

S: *Why?*

J: The lobotomy had done something to my brain. They had hit so much that…and this was not a precise surgery. This was something that was equivalent to sticking a hand blender up my nose. I couldn't lift my head up. I felt like I was just hunched over, and I had trouble walking at first. It got better over the next couple of weeks, but I couldn't remember a majority of my life anymore. I couldn't remember the television station where I worked, or my mom, or Julie. But I was very sharp. I could still understand the lives I'd had before. And I began to understand more during this time. I could remember my life in Lemuria and my other lives before that and what I had seen and had come to understand about all of it. I lived in THAT world. I could not get out of it; I could not speak. I couldn't express it to anybody anymore, and it was so clear in my mind that it had closed off this door to the outside of me, but it had opened the door to the inside of me. It pushed me further within myself and I could see so much, and I could do so much within, but I could not help the outer part of myself. My physical body was now incapacitated, and I was now a prisoner within myself once again. But I began to see more. I could go where I wanted to go, and it helped me get away from the torture, the molestation, and the disgusting place I was in. And it got me through that, until I was able to get myself out of there one day and end my life once and for all.

CHAPTER 11: A SOLAR FLASH THAT MANY STILL REMEMBER

With many people wondering about the possibility of a solar flash coming to Earth it was interesting to find out through my sessions with Jen that many of us remember experiencing one before. Below is Jen's recount of a solar flash that many still remember.

S: What did you notice when you went further into yourself after the lobotomy?

J: I could go deeper into myself after the lobotomy, and I remembered more about what life was like on our home planet during other existences. There was a time before our civilization was as enlightened as it had been when I was a commander.

S: What was life like on your home planet before the civilization had evolved?

J: It feels very similar to a simpler time in Earth's history here, like the 1950s, before people became more evolved and advanced. People on my home planet at that time were searching for some kind of perfection that they couldn't find. There was a period of time where our systems broke down and that breakdown allowed us to evolve into the next phase. And through this process of evolution, we began to slow down our birth rate and our ability to reproduce. As that evolvement progressed, it eventually transcended until reproduction was no longer necessary.

S: What caused this breakdown of perfection?

J: There was a bright solar flash that came to the planet. It looked similar to an asteroid coming to Earth creating a big flash. There was a big bright light that gently grazed the planet and when the energy of it hit our planet, it created change.

S: Do you know where this solar flash came from?

J: It had been summoned by our people. It was an orchestrated arrival on a very different cellular level.

S: You said that it created change when this solar flash came. Did people feel anything when that light came?

J: There was a lot of shock and awe at first, then a breaking down of the image of perfection.

S: *How did this light break down the image of perfection?*

J: This light quickly allowed all to see themselves very clearly, it was humbling.

S: *After the light came what happened next?*

J: After the flash it was a quick acceleration mentally for these people on my planet, and at first, they felt distraught.

S: *Why did they feel distraught?*

J: They realized that so much had to be broken down in their society in order to evolve.

S: *Tell me more.*

J: Many fought this at first, it wasn't something that everyone wanted. Many felt comfortable in this perfection they were striving for and felt that the perfection would lead to their evolution. But it wasn't the perfection of their society that would lead to their evolution, it was the breakdown of their society that led to their evolution and allowed them to progress to eventually become the visitors and seeders of Earth. They hit the same place of evolution that we are currently in, a very long time before they came to Earth to seed this planet.

S: *Can you tell me more about when they hit where we are evolutionarily? What makes you say that's where we are?*

J: Because we are at an evolutionary jumping point, and that is where they were as well. Though the two events are not the same, they do have similarities in that what Earth is going through now is a jumping point in its evolution. The end results will not be identical, but it is still the instigating factor of what creates this evolution of life on planets. These things need to occur.

S: *Why do they need to occur exactly?*

J: If they don't, then things become stagnant. And when things are stagnant nothing progresses.
S: *So, this evolutionary point has to occur on planets?*

J: It has to occur at several points. What is happening on Earth now will not be the first or the last. There will eventually be a point on Earth where we will hit an ultimate evolutionary point and the planet will no longer be necessary.

S: *How long from now do you see that happening?*

J: Millions of years. This takes a long time to accomplish. We will not see our Earthy bodies evolve to the point we were in during the end days of the home planet.

S: What about when you lived as the commander on your home planet. What point in your planet's evolution was that?

J: Three quarters of the way done. It had already progressed greatly from the flash that occurred when I lived as the commander. Approximately one hundred thousand years had passed from that solar flash at that point.

S: What type of technology or advancements took away the ability to reproduce?

J: It was a natural progression over time. When there is no longer a need to eat, there is also no longer a need to reproduce. These are things our bodies need when our minds work on a lower vibrational level. But as we progress and evolve, we no longer need to perform these functions in order to create the world around us, and that is where we are at right now. We are not ready yet for that type of evolutionary jump where we don't need to eat. When we get to this type of evolutionary jump there won't even be a need for our feet to touch the floor; we will not need to transport ourselves in that manner even.

S: Before the solar flash did your people eat food?

J: While these are collective memories and do not belong just to me, but most living on Earth as well at this time, they did eat food at one point. But like I said, as they evolved, they moved past those needs once their bodies transformed. It took a long time for this to happen, and this was a cumulative result over years and eons.

S: What did their food look like?

J: The food looked like dark red pudding that was eaten out of metal bowls. It was very nutrient rich, and it had different flavors as you ate it. It would start off with a very minerally flavored texture and taste, but as it melted in your mouth it would get sweeter and become more liquidly as it would dissolve. You could put some of this food under your tongue because it was so nutrient dense, and it helped you to boost this life-giving source that people during that time needed. Before the solar flash this food was mass produced and given to many people. But after the flash they stopped needing to eat, and these nutrients were then administrated to people.

S: What did these people look like during this time?

J: They look very pale and iridescent. I don't know a word for this luminescent skin they have. They look almost ethereal.

S: Did they wear clothes or no?

J: They wore clothes at points in their history, but they evolved to a point where there became no need for it. Their bodies were different than humans in that there was no definition to the body. The body itself was still a dimensional being but it didn't have the same type of organs or skin that humans have. As they evolved, their shape changed even more into something that was way more advanced.

They became a whitish grey over time with what looks almost like the stars of the Universe within their skin in a way. There was a vibrancy to them.

S: Was there a masculine and feminine energy before the solar flash, before this change?

J: There was, but there was also a lot of repression there. They were always searching for perfection before this flash and in their search for perfection their society also became exclusionary, pushing out those who weren't part of their perfection. During this time before the solar flash many were very close minded, with a two genders and black and white mindset.

S: What type of people did they push out? Why did they push those people out?

J: It was more of a push to conformity, to be part of this perfect society that they were aiming for. This stopped after the flash and people were no longer finding themselves needing this perfection. After the flash they started to find themselves within themselves. They were able to look at themselves, find themselves, and begin the inward journey that evolves people through the mind. The barriers they had set for themselves were lifted from around their minds with this flash, and after that, they were able to start absorbing this new understanding of themselves and the world around them.

S: Many people have talked about a flash coming here to Earth. Will this happen here as well?

J: Yes, but this will be a slow progression and not a quick one as it was on our home planet. This energy that came to our planet was a white flash, the energy coming to Earth now is a whiteish-blue light. It is similar but it is different. It is an improvement because at each level of this experiment we improve upon things, and we find better ways to perform and to accelerate our expansion. And the white light was useful there for what was needed, but the blue light is more useful here on Earth for what is needed for our evolvement here.

S: Why blue?

J: The blue draws us back to the memories we store within ourselves of the blue planet. The white draws us back to memories of an even earlier time before the blue planet.

S: What are the memories of the blue planet?

J: For many that was the color of the home planet. It was blue, but you can also see a red and a blue planet from the blue planet, just like you can see the moon from Earth. The home planet was similar to Earth in that the Earth also has a blue atmosphere because of the water that is located here. The blue of the home planet is a different type of blue, a more vibrant blue than the blue for this Earth. Earth's blue is a darker blue.

S: Did people eat animals on the home planet?

J: Once they evolved to a certain point they didn't; it wasn't necessary; they grew out of it.

S: They did in the beginning?

J: In earlier times it looks like there were animals that were similar to rabbits that were bigger and were highly prized as food.

S: Did they have any of the red crystals on the home planet?

J: Yes, they did not understand these crystals for a very long time, and with the flash the memory of the red crystals from their even earlier home planet began to awaken.

S: What were those memories?

J: The memories of the red crystals were very mathematical. People were given these understandings of how to use the red crystals, but the information was very binary. The information involved lots of coding that was implanted to them, and they were also implanted with ideas when they held these crystals and used them. And that allowed them to understand how to build things and how to create and scientifically advance their society as well. They were able to hold onto these red crystals in a way in which they remembered, after the flash, that allowed for this progression to happen. They quickly advanced their society as a result of these innovations.

S: Are there any red crystals on our Earth planet now? If so, where are they?

J: They are hidden, but some I see within a cave underneath the Atlantic Ocean, hidden far, far down below, somewhere between us and Africa.

S: You said before that the Mermaids took the crystals and hid them away.

J: They did. The Mermaids were witness to the abuse and the genetic alterations of the humans they had befriended in early Atlantis. They sought to free the humans from the Atlantean rule, but it was too late. The humans had already been changed too greatly. The Mermaids tried and could not save their friends so they took what they could of the crystals and hid them away.

S: Was there a reason why they hid them in caves?

J: They understood that only people of their kind would be able to go and recover them at the depth they went.

S: Will these red crystals stay in these caves? Are they used for anything now?

J: The red crystals are better left hidden there because there is not a **human alive that is ready to digest the power of the red crystals and use it for the betterment of this planet.** We're not at that evolutionary point where we are selfless beings that will use it for this great advancement. Until we hit that point the power and ability of these red crystals will always drag us down.

S: Will it ever again be used on this Earth?

J: There will be a point in the future where there will be recurrences of it, but it doesn't seem to be any time soon. It looks like it will be well into the future.

S: *What about the Mermaids? Are they still evolving?*

J: There isn't a strong evolution for them. They are very small in numbers, and they are content in their ways and prefer to have an isolated existence free of human intervention.

S: *Tell me more about your other memories after the lobotomy?*

J: I remember I would go deeper into my memory of the place you would call **Antarctica** because it brought me so much joy. My memories of Antarctica were memories of green fields with small rolling hills. I see children running around these large dome-like structures, these silver dome like structures that are all in this one area on this green hill side. I just loved these memories, especially the ones of these hybrid children.

S: *What do these children look like?*

J: They are very pale, but they have hair. Some are short with very dark curly hair and very tight curls. Others have a very light silvery colored hair. Those are the two variations I see of these children. It is a mix of the humans that were left to evolve on their own for a time and the visitors that have come to work with these genetics. There are a lot of children there. They are all running around these dome structures playing, chasing each other. They don't have short hair, it's all long. They let their hair grow because it gave them some sort of power to have long hair, but I can't see exactly why.

S: *Anything else you notice about these children?*

J: It looks like school, but it's more than school. It's like they are taking the children out, so they run off their energy. They're teaching them the ways of the home planet. They're teaching them how to communicate and meditate. They are trying to make them into these naturally advanced beings. But it's taken time, and the scientists that have come to teach them are not used to the rambunctiousness of children. They are used to the more advanced society that does not have children. It can be very challenging in their experiment, but the human helpers that they have there are very good at this. They are very nurturing and family oriented and very much a unit.

S: *What happens to these children after they are schooled?*

J: Some of them are taken and spread out to other colonies. Antarctica was used for many things, but I remember it as a place of transformation. These children don't stay there for their entire lives. They will be born there and raised there, but in their early teenage years, they are removed and taken to another colony where they are added. This (school) was not a colony meant to continue on its own; this is just where they housed the original genetic breeding program.

S: *When these hybrids were taken to other colonies what happened?*

J: They are left with the other colonists in these colonies, and they are sent there with these advancements to help the human colonies grow and prosper. The children are prepared their entire lives to be a gift that is given to these colonies, and these children are very humble, peaceful beings of joy. They are full of good intentions and good ideas. And they are meant to bring these communities together, and to bring them advancements, to spread knowledge, and to help evolve the communities.

S: Do the communities know who they are and that these children are special?

J: They have an understanding of what is going on when the children are brought to them. They know that there is a mix between the two races and that these children are special and have powers. The people look at them as a demigod, they are part visitor from the stars and part human, and they are seen as special and to be revered and used as guidance.

S: Could you tell me more about the legends of hybrid beings throughout history?

J: There is confusion about what these hybrid beings were and the powers that they had. There was not enough experience for these early humans to understand truly what they were and sometimes the hybrid children were interpreted only as a God, in ways that made sense to these early humans and made them feel protected and safe. Sometimes for the early humans the belief around these children gave them something to believe in because they were so magical, and something to hope for. There was the hope that these hybrids and occasionally otherworldly visitors would continue to help, guide, and give the humans things that they needed, and to solve things that they couldn't solve on their own. The hybrid children throughout the ages have caused confusion because they had bodies that would look similar to a human, but they would also have certain differences to make them stand out, and they would have otherworldly abilities or knowledge. And that is why they sometimes were thought of mistakenly as a God.

CHAPTER 12: UNDERGROUND TUNNELS

As we were progressing through Jen's memories after the lobotomy, interesting information about underground tunnels started to emerge.

S: Is there anything else about Antarctica that seems important?

J: There is a large facility underneath Antarctica that is still underground. There is a large rectangular door that is built into a rock wall, and it looks very monolithic with a dark reddish-brown color to it and made out of a type of metal. I can't see into it, but I know there is stuff there that has been left there.

S: What kind of stuff is underneath the ice in Antarctica?

J: It looks like ships that they came over on. Antarctica was a storage facility that is now covered in so much snow and ice at the moment. It is still there but has been hidden away for a very long time.

S: Will the snow and ice ever melt and allow people to see what is there?

J: We will see more glimpses and tips of possibility, but in our lifetime, we will not be able to go into these facilities, these storage facilities from our ancient ancestors. This will take an event that would be very catastrophic, and we feel it is better not done in this existence.

S: Are there other colonies on other planets that have been seeded by your home planet?

J: There are. They are far away from Earth; there are about seven of them that I see.

S: What are these planets like?

J: They have evolved slightly differently than Earth. There is one that has less water and more snow, and it looks whiter on the outside. At this time, they are in more of an ice age at the top of their planet. There is more ice and whiteness to their planet, and they look like they are at a very basic time right now in their development. They live within these cave systems, but it is only for a time, for a few generations, and only during their ice age that they will be in these underground cave systems. The tunnel systems keep them safe as they understood that this ice age was going to happen. There is something within their solar system that was predicted to be off kilter and cause this freezing event. And they prepared by digging out these tunnels. When my mind had no limits after the lobotomy, I could look into any direction I wanted. And I remember looking deeper into the ice age on this Earth.

S: Can you tell me what happened to this Earth during this Earth's ice age?

J: There were tunnels that were made in a lighter clay, a cream-colored clay wall that they chiseled through. These tunnels just go on and on, and even now are still very strong.

S: They're still there?

J: Yes, the underground tunnels within the Earth are still there, and it looks like they go on and on and can cross countries.

S: Did the inhabitants of this Earth have warning? What were the tunnels for?

J: There was a warning, an intervention. Visitors came and warned the humans about the freezing of the planet and told them to build these underground places.

S: Who built these places?

J: The visitors gave the people advanced tools and drilling devices. The people were able to use the advanced equipment while being guided by the visitors.

S: Why did the visitors give them these tools and warn them?

J: The visitors did not want their experiment to disappear.

S: Can you tell me more about these tools?

J: They looked like cylinders with a very sharp point to it. It was held by both hands. It looks like a copper rod with a V that sticks out the back of it. The people would hold on to this device and chisel around and make these structures and these smooth cavernous walls. They also had guidance from these tools as to where to chisel. They were guided within the cavernous walls where natural caverns were, and these advanced tools guided them to these. It wasn't blind luck in them drilling smaller tunnels and finding these larger caverns to build these communities in.

S: What happened to those tools after they were used?

J: Some were taken back; others are still there at the very bottoms of the caves. As they completed this drilling, they would leave them there and cover them.

S: How long did people live in these communities and what was that like?

J: For hundreds if not a thousand years.

S: *When some of the Lemurians who had escaped the destruction of their land went to Mt. Shasta did they build the tunnels because they had done this before or were those tunnels already there?*

J: There were tunnels within Mt. Shasta that were already there from earlier colonists, however, there were some tunnels within Mt. Shasta that were specifically made in preparation for the ice age that came to this planet after the fall of Atlantis.

S: *Tell me more about that. Was this right after Atlantis was destroyed?*

J: This wasn't something that happened immediately after the destruction of Atlantis, but possibly a thousand years later perhaps. However, the visitors were very instrumental in helping the societies prepare and begin a civilization underground, and the visitors even taught these societies how to adapt to this as well. This was not done quickly or even overnight, and it took a considerable amount of time to usher people into these cities. It was meant to be a long term, well thought out intervention against the ice shelf that was coming.

S: *Can you tell me more about the tunnels in Mt Shasta?*

J: Their experiment there was to create this safe ground for people to be in when the ice arrived and when it began to cover everything. There was a need to create another civilization that was self-reliant under the ground, under the mountain.

S: *Tell me more.*

J: A very large civilization underground within Mt. Shasta began at this time. Unfortunately, this civilization also had many difficulties during the time of hibernation with many wanting to leave and revolt, but there was nowhere to go when they were all frozen in.

S: *Tell me more about that.*

J: They were frozen in and had to stay within these tunnels. There was no way to leave, and they had to wait it out for generations before the ice even melts. At that point when it does begin to recede and reveal this landscape of beauty again, these people have forgotten many parts of themselves. They forgot parts of themselves during this long time period of isolation. Some leave after the ice leaves and they never return back to the mountain, and some stay. A small community stays within the mountain, within Mt. Shasta, in California. The others who leave integrate back into society and interbreed and become part of us. But there are people who are still feeling the pull towards that mountain because it is in their genes and their blood, having lived through that time of isolation during the ice age. Or for some they remember the escape from Lemuria and their days spent during that harrowing time and in that city underground.

S: *They feel a pull towards Mt Shasta?*

J: Yes, they can't understand why, but it's because their genealogy is there, their family is there, their other parts of themselves are there.

S: If they go there, will they feel anything?

J: Many will feel a feeling of completion in what that energy and that mountain brings back to them if they go to Mt. Shasta. For some it is a feeling of going home, though they will not see their home there, but just know and feel that it is there on a very deep level.

S: So, for these people, is it enough to just go to this mountain?

J: By being on it or even just around it is enough to feel the energy that is there from the earliest times until after the ice age. It is still pulling people towards it, there was too much humanity there for it not to have that pull.

S: Tell me more.

J: A civilization leaves an imprint. A part of that imprint can be carried by you for a very long time and other parts of this imprint can even be part of something bigger. You are part of this connectivity to all of these parts, and these are the things that help you understand that while you are part of something much bigger you are also part of many smaller things as well. And everything in this Universe just comes together to become this oneness that is us.

S: Was there a purpose for the ice age, or a reason why it happened?

J: Things felt as if they were beginning to get out of control again after the fall of Atlantis, and there needed to be a balance restored.

S: Why an ice age?

J: It was to help the Earth rebalance.

S: How did it help the Earth rebalance?

J: It helped to get rid of the colonies that were no longer serving the experiment, those that had been too corrupted by the power or the memory of the red crystals. So many experiments went wrong, not wrong, but just not what we needed. However, there was always a need for variance. The variables of the experiment created many outcomes and versions of humans, but not all humans became pleasant, evolved people. Some became very brutal and evil.

S: Those had to be destroyed?

J: Yes, to protect the future of humanity and to try to preserve the humans that were closest to the goal of evolvement that we were searching for here on Earth. Too much had gone wrong in other communities. There was too much that could not be solved. They needed to have intervention, so it was a galactic intervention. They were breeding hatred and creating a wave of hatred towards each other, moving us further and further away from our goal of reconnection and evolvement.

S: Were there many who passed during the ice age because they didn't have the shelter of the caves?

J: Yes, many communities were destroyed and covered by ice, landslides or even mud.

S: Tell me more.

J: I see one particular civilization that was destroyed very clearly. This civilization was on an island in the North Atlantic around Ireland. But the world looked differently than what it does now.

S: How did it look different then?

J: The Earth had more water in places. A large portion of England and Europe were all underwater.

S: Why was this civilization destroyed?

J: There is a battle for control and power between this divine feminine energy and this brute Viking, Atlantean energy.

S: Tell me more about that. Does the battle begin before or after the ice age?

J: This was just one of the instigating factors in the beauty of the ice age and the freezing of everything over. **It was literally a cool down period.** Things had become too hot tempered and too overwhelming. Everything was too explosive, and the ice age was a perfect way to calm this and to give the Earth time to heal, sleep, and allow us to redo this again. Things had become very sparce in some places after Atlantis. After Atlantis it was discussed amongst the collective consciousness that if something like what happened in Atlantis or Lemuria should ever happen again then there should be a protective measure to ensure that we should not let so many people die. Death did not solve the problem. There were so many who died and allowing those souls to reincarnate creates even more of the karmic debt that affects our energy and affects the pull of these karmic debts that comes to us.

S: So, after the destruction of Atlantis, what exactly was decided?

J: The decision was made that they should not let such a level of destruction happen again because it creates too much of this karma that fogs the way the energy around us works.

S: Tell me more about that.

J: The karmic energy can hold people to these places where they experienced the trauma and to this trauma itself. And while it's important to remember these events and places in certain ways the time we are in now is ripe to release this trauma in this current environment. The souls that perished during those two major cataclysms carried so much of that karma and trauma that it has affected how long it will take for us to hit our next evolutionary point.

S: So, the destructions of Atlantis and Lemuria have affected this?

J: Yes, because the destructions created more of this gumminess that we need to shed and work past, in order to get back to our true selves.

S: How do you shed the gumminess?

J: By working through it. It is something that when we leave our physical bodies we do take into account, when we are in the in-between, when we are being shown and reviewing our lives and planning our next existence. The traumas we haven't released affect how we plan out our next existence and the more of it we can remove during our incarnation really allows us to open up different opportunities.

S: How does a person remove their trauma so that they can move past it?

J: By facing it. A total remembering though is not needed. This is one of the reasons why you are writing this book. Through the art of reading, one may recognize and release these traumas, or start the process of this healing. And your book is the perfect catalyst for that.

S: Anything else about this that is important?

J: All of this information is stored and broadcast from the Sphinx.

S: Did the Sphinx lose any power during the ice age?

J: No, it has been surrounded by many different elements, snow, water, ice, flooding, dryness, and it is still in the shape that it is in because it was built with such longevity of technology. The technology used to build the Sphinx was something more advanced than we are used to building with now. And it was also built in the right place and all of these things allowed it to be persevered against weatherization.

S: Do you notice anything else about this advanced technology that the Sphinx has?

J: No, but **there was a visitor who came down at one point who went by the name Three**, like I had said before. And he came trying to show people and educate them about the Sphinx. He's like a teacher when it comes to this information; he understands what is in the Sphinx. A part of him in a previous incarnation was one of the people who built the Sphinx and put this momentum into the Sphinx. So, he knows the real history of the Sphinx and the secrets within it. He has come back in order to help these people understand this better. He/It has come back and is here again now. He has information about the Sphinx.

S: You said that after the lobotomy that you could look anywhere inside of yourself. Was there anything else that you noticed?

J: The lobotomy gave me an ability to explore and go wherever I wanted. I noticed that there were big pockets within the Earth that are hollow; there are massive cave systems and tunnels that have been covered and many of the entrances have been filled in over time.

S: Tell me more.

J: After my lobotomy I would often explore my memories of Antarctica, as I have said. It brought me much joy. Antarctica is a solid land mass, but there are still many underground facilities underneath the ice there.

S: What about the sightings of giants? I heard that they lived inside the Earth, in tunnels, is this true?

J: These tunnels seem very big, almost unreal, so that is possible. There is a secondary natural source of light down there.

S: Tell me more.

J: I'm looking really far down within a large cavern, deep within the Earth. The walls look like they are curved and smoothed out. There is light coming in, but it's not coming in from the sun. I see green growing moss on things, and it looks like there is sunlight shining down onto it in the distance, in the center of this room, center of this cavern. It does have this strange light beaming down on it, but it doesn't look like the sunlight we have here.

S: How does it look different?

J: This light bounces in a way and it looks like it dances and moves around like a beam coming from somewhere. It isn't a light source; it looks more like a covered dome with light inside of it. Within this deep cavern though this light looks like it is a yellowish color. It feels like sun when I stand underneath it and I see that this light can also grows things.

S: What does it grow?

J: Algae and moss on the rocks. It feels dry and not slippery.

S: Are there any beings there at all, or no?

J: It looks like this cavern that I'm looking at was a gathering place for people. It looks abandoned now, but at one time this was where they would meet together.

S: What would they do there?

J: They would come together and learn from one another, within these tunnels. They would eat different things as well. They would take different kinds of mushrooms and algae, and things like that, and show different ways of using them. It was an exchange of ideas in this large cavern.

S: Are there any giant humans, or no?

J: I see that there are, but they are shy and more likely to keep to themselves because of their size. They can feel very out of place at times. Many of them have chosen to stay within the caves because they enjoy the comforts of the cave. They find this encapsulation comforting, and the outside world very threatening, and too open and exposing.

S: Why are they giant?

J: Just like the Mermaids, they were a product of the hybridization experimentation that happened early on when seeding this Earth.

S: Tell me more.

J: Some humans were made into giants to help their communities.

S: Why?

J: The colonizers brought many different genetics here from other parts of the Universe, to see if having larger humans would help with building and protection. The colonizers wanted to see if the larger humans would help those who couldn't protect themselves. So, they created these, what you would call giants, in order to make life here on Earth easier. But it became a threat instead of a help, and the group of giant humans sought to hide within the Earth is what I see from this perspective. They were hunted by the same people they were meant to protect, because they were seen as a threat. It looks like there was much violence against them. Those that still exist appear to live within these caverns that are within the Earth. They are able to construct these tunnels themselves, and these tunnels all connect, and underneath Antarctica looks like it used to be one convergence point. There are many different beings that live within the Earth, but there are certain places where some of them meet, converge, and share their ideas. The convergence point is where they learn from each other and get updates on what is happening in the outside world.

S: So, underneath Antarctica was a convergence point?

J: Underneath Antarctica was, but it looks abandoned now. However, there are others that are still active underneath the ground, all over the Earth.

S: Where are the other convergence points, can you see?

J: There is one underneath the United States that goes all the way to central America and down into south America. There are some that go all throughout the middle east. That whole area seems to be filled with these underground tunnels and convergence points. I see them in Turkey, China, up to Mongolia, and into Europe.

S: Why are there tunnels under the Sphinx? Are they connected, or no?

J: There are, but that is sealed off.

S: *Why?*

J: You can get to a certain point, but you can't use the tunnels up to the Sphinx. The beings who use these tunnels understand what is underneath the Sphinx, and they know that it is not for them. Humanity is meant to uncover this information at a later point, and they are respectful of that.

S: *Can you tell me what is there?*

J: Some of what is hidden under the Sphinx is technology that was left over from our ancient ancestors, the first who came here to settle Earth. This technology would be hard to explain as it would so obviously show the link to our origins beyond the stars, but it is not meant for us to encounter just yet. We have much evolvement to undertake before our brains can comprehend what this means and how to use this, and what this links us back to.

S: *Who hides this?*

J: We have hidden this from ourselves over many, many generations and we have lost this information because we have had to hide this from others. It was never an easy road to bring everyone to this understanding and consensus. And it has taken us a very long time to begin to get there. And that is part of what the Sphinx is there for, it is there for confirmation when we do get to this point. We will have that there to show us. And it is not the only place where this technology has been hidden, it is in other places as well.

S: *Where else is this hidden?*

J: Under Mt. Shasta, California. There is a lot of technology there as well, down within, deep within.

S: *About how deep?*

J: Miles and miles deep.

S: *Is there anything else that's interesting that is within that mountain?*

J: There is a very bright and powerful orb of light very deep within.

S: *What is this orb of light exactly?*

J: It is the information, similar to the information within the Sphinx, the connection back to our past, our planet, and our existence.

S: *What does this information entail?*

J: If you touch this light within the Sphinx and immerse yourself into this light, it will fully awaken you.

S: What exactly would you remember if you did that?

J: Where we came from and why we are here, and what life is for the individual who encounters it. But this light will be fully understood closer to the extinction of this planet. It will be one of the final legs of our journey here.

S: What will this planet's extinction be like?

J: Many will leave, and we will continue to seed new plants. During the final extinction of Earth, it looks like a beautiful explosion that levels everything out, like a drop of water into the ocean with the ripples that emanate from that drop. It explodes and implodes everything before it flattens out into nothing.

S: At the extinction point will there be a civilization still living here, and if so, do they know that the extinction is coming?

J: It seems like they will know what they are doing. They will have hit a higher evolutionary point where they no longer need food or have a need for reproduction. When they hit that point, they will know that it is time to go.

S: When will people hit that point?

J: Millions of years from now possibly. It is very far off.

CHAPTER 13: THE AFTERLIFE

I'm always curious when it comes to my client's recounts of death and the afterlife. I was interested to learn more about the final moments of Christie's life.

S: Why did you want to end that life after your lobotomy? Did you still have awareness of what was happening to you there inside the mental facility?

J: Even though I couldn't remember much of my life, I knew that there was no way to complete my mission, and I understood that. I could see so much but I couldn't express anything, it was trapped within me. There was no way they were ever going to let me out of there.

S: So, you knew this, and that is why you were ready to leave?

J: No one would trust the word of a woman who had been lobotomized. And I knew this, I knew it was over.

S: How long were you there? How did you escape?

J: I feel like I'm there for two to three months until I'm able to escape one day. I remember I didn't have shoes on. They don't give you shoes for the simple reason that they didn't want anyone to try to escape. But after my lobotomy no one felt the need to watch over me as much. I remember the gown I wore. It was blue and it had a small darker blue curlicue pattern to it. My hair was a mess. It's all greasy and unbrushed.

S: Tell me more.

J: It feels that they have shaved off parts of my hair, and I'm missing a big portion on the top.

S: Why?

J: They shaved a part of my head when they took out a part of my brain.

S: What happens next?

J: I knew there was one thing left to do. I knew this life for me was over and that I wouldn't be able to complete the mission as I had wanted. So, one night I was able to escape, and as I did, I found the bridge. I knew that I needed to end this life. I went to the middle of the bridge and slid over the side. I remember the freezing cold side of the bridge as I slid off.

S: Tell me more.

J: I remember the light on the bridge flashing. This was the Brooklyn bridge as I can see it very clearly. I remember the lights on the bridge creating what looked almost like a little light show for me as I jumped down. I felt that feeling of falling in my stomach, and that feeling stays with me, it stays with me always. As I started falling, I noticed that **there's this crazy energy that goes through your body when you're about to die.**

S: What is this energy like?

J: This energy shoots from my toes all the way up to every hair on my head. It feels exhilarating and exciting, it's not a terrible feeling. It's unbelievable this excitement that comes from it. The feeling is an exhilaration of freedom. The best way to describe it is like an overwhelming feeling of relief that you are finally free, and free of this body.

S: Do you feel this as you die, or before?

J: As you're dying.

S: Tell me more about this death process?

J: It feels freeing, that is the best way to explain it. I feel the freest I've ever felt in my life. I feel no pain, no constraints, no judgement, no trauma, nothing but freedom and exhilaration. But then I feel myself stop and I'm pulled. I feel like I'm pulled back and suddenly interrupted and I'm upset because I want to keep feeling this freedom.

S: Why was it stopped?

J: Because they have pulled me out of that body, and I no longer have the weight, or the same feelings of that body now. And then I stop, and I watch the body drop down and splash into the water before it disappears.

S: What was that like to watch that? Do you feel anything as you do?

J: There is a mixed feeling to it. Because I feel that I loved her, and I loved that body. And I wanted so much more for her, but she couldn't have it. She couldn't continue to live like that. She couldn't continue to live or complete her mission after they took that piece of her brain out. But I'm also hit with the regret of taking this life, it wasn't what was intended, and the sudden realization that I will have to repeat this mission floods my soul.

S: So, you have to repeat this mission? Do you get a sense as to what the purpose of that lifetime was now that you're out of the body?

J: Yes, I am repeating this now as Jen. The purpose of that life as Christie was to begin this process of bringing this information forward, but it was not the right time. It was too early, too ahead of its time. The world was not ready to begin hearing that yet. They are ready for this information now!

S: Was there anything that you wish you had done instead of jumping off the bridge?

J: It was not supposed to end with my suicide. There was still a plan that needed to be completed. There was a plan that was unfinished.

S: How was it supposed to end?

J: There was a version of my life where it could've ended differently. In this other version of my life, instead of presenting it to people before I fully understood it, I was supposed to digest it and write it down. Not just presenting it to people who were looking to harm me and judge my own existence based on their reaction to this information I was sharing with them. I needed to do things in a way where I could've digested this information first before I let it out!

S: Why did you choose to come into such a beautiful person's body then?

J: The plan had been that I would be attractive to make it easier to bring this message to people. If I were a presentable person or if I were physically attractive, then there would be more of an attraction to the message. But, instead, it created a series of problems that took its own direction.

S: Tell me more.

J: I believe the true death happened when they took a part of my brain out, that was the final indicator that what I had planned for this life was not going to happen in that lifetime.

S: Was there any pain at all when you jumped off the bridge?

J: I didn't feel any pain, but I felt the feeling of plummeting and the cold. I didn't feel myself die.

S: After you left the body, what happened?

J: I feel that they pull me up and when they do, I'm instantly warm. I feel comforted with what feels like a light around me, protecting me, as if I'm in a bubble of this light that is surrounding me and lifting me up.

S: As they lift you up are you aware of what just happened? Do you have awareness?

J: I feel more awareness than I did in a human body, I know exactly what just happened. However, I feel very sleepy in this bubble of protection. I feel like I'm just being put to sleep and suspended in something far above us. It seems as if I'm there only for a short amount of time.

S: When you're asleep do you have any awareness or no?

J: Not really, it feels like a very deep process that is more than the sleep we have here. It's almost like a coma without anything around you or anything to absorb while you're in that state.

S: What happens to you while you're in that state?

J: You're rested in every way possible. Your soul is rested. It's such a deep rest that it is meant to rest the soul in order for it afterwards to be able to clearly look at the life it just finished and understand it. The soul needs a moment to clear, to rest, and to just be settled before you begin to go over your previous existence, and before you are able to understand where you are now, and what has happened in that life to your soul.

S: After you rest and clear your soul, what did you notice?

J: It feels like the light just dissipates away from you and you begin to look around at your surroundings. It is very comfortable, there is a lightness to it and a calmness. I would equate it to watching the sunset or like being in a room full of clouds. It just feels calm and settling. And it feels like something has ended, but it is good, and it is beautiful. You are not alone there. There is another presence there with you. I have seen this before, it's funny how I'm remembering how I've done this so many times before! This presence has the shape of a body, but it looks as if it is really the Universe within this body. It is filled with what looks like galaxies and stars. It has a shape, and it moves, but it moves in a fluid motion, like water. It is this expressionless void with a shape of a body. It's larger than a human's body, but it just feels like a larger presence than what our bodies are on this planet.

S: Does this presence say anything to you?

J: It doesn't say anything, but I know why it's there. It's there because we are going to view the life that I just lived, from the moment I left this in-between place, to when I came back. And we are going to look at it together because we are one in the same. It is a continuation of me that has come back to join me to review this.

S: Tell me more about this part of you.

J: This is the part of me that doesn't go into the earthly body. This is the part of me that remains. And we are going to review my life together.

S: What is the review like?

J: I know I have done this many times before as I'm doing it again here. These memories are coming back very quickly. You begin to process your life, and from this perspective it feels as if you aren't as attached to it as you would be when you were alive. You remember everything though. You remember who you really are and what has happened. And you remember what the goals were that you set up for yourself in that life. In this in-between place you have a different understanding of yourself, and an overwhelming love for yourself. When you look at it from that way, you really love that person that you were. The love is so strong here. The only word we have for that feeling is love, but I know it is more than just our concept of love, it's just so much deeper. This is the same feeling of overwhelming universal love that people feel when they are in trance or when they have near death experiences. It's that same feeling, and I feel there should be a better word for it, but that is the closest we have.

S: Is there anything about the review that looks interesting?

J: I knew that this life that I chose to come into in the nineteen seventies may be too early to begin this process and share this information. But I was Impatient, and I insisted that this would be the right thing to try out, that I was ready to try it. And I feel that there was a knowingness that there could be a chance that this information would not be ready. I insisted anyway. I tried, and I failed. But there is no failure, really, in any of this. There will just be the next time.

S: Do you plan out the next time?

J: As soon as we are done viewing that life we begin working on the next. We begin looking at the different scenarios that exist for me to come back and try this again in the next life.

S: What are those scenarios?

J: I'm told I could come back sooner if I would like, but I choose not to. I choose to float for a few more years. I want to float and see things change first before I come back. I don't want to come back right away; I don't think it's exactly time yet to do so.

S: What did you choose?

J: I see the opportunities for this life I'm in as Jen. This life would work not only with that other lifetime in the seventies, but the lifetime before it as well. This lifetime as Jen links up to people that I will be born to that will settle what looks like karma from other lifetimes. It looks like a perfect scenario for me, and I wait around a few more years in the resting place for this. I wait for this lifetime that I'm in now. They (the helpers on the other side) knew that this perfect life would be coming up, and if I was patient and willing to float for some time, the timing would be right. And when this time was right to share this information I would come back into a body, into this perfect life from which to share this information.

S: Is this the body that you're in now?

J: This is the current body, yes.

S: What did you choose for this life?

J: To meet with you. To uncover this information and to share it with as many people as possible, as the world has been waiting. The world needs and is ready for this information now. This information itself has a consciousness. It is meant to help humanity at this time. It is interesting looking at this information from this perspective. The information itself will find its way to those searching for it.

S: Tell me more about what you planned for this current life as Jen.

J: I feel like when I plan this life, that before I do, I'm in what looks to me like a rounded lecture hall.

S: Tell me more about it.

J: It looks like a room made out of white alabaster where the walls are smooth and cold to the touch but it's also very modern looking. There's a lot of natural light coming in from a circular opening at the top, creating what looks like a very beautiful floaty light that pulsates down. The light floats down to the ground; it doesn't shine down.

S: How do you feel in this place?

J: Very light, free, and full of this love. I'm easily able to float around and maneuver. There are levels in this place. I don't feel that I have a body or hunger, or the need to sleep, or any ailments whatsoever. It almost feels like you are just a set of eyes and a brain. There's nothing physical there, but you can still perceive what is happening around you as if you were seeing. And you can still register thought. And in some ways, you can even still touch and feel things, if you choose to. This is the resting place.

S: What exactly is the resting place?

J: It's an interesting place. You can go and float around and look at things, like different aspects of history. There is so much here that you can spend a lot of time looking at everything. And because this place is made up of levels, you can go and float up to a level where you feel comfortable.

S: What do you mean by levels?

J: In this place you are floating. And as you float up to the circular part of the ceiling it can bring you to different levels of your existence. This place holds your eternal beingness, the history that is you. And you can review other parts of your existence there.

S: Is there anything interesting about your particular levels of existence?

J: There is a lot! There are many levels here; it all feels so familiar as I scan through a lot of this and feel these feelings. The levels are meant to help you as you are resting; it's meant to bring you reassurance and act as a reminder of your ascensions.

S: What do you mean by that, act as a reminder of your ascensions?

J: Each level that you are shown within this rounded room is a different ascension point of your many existences. And it doesn't matter where, or when, or how, or even what you looked like, or what language you spoke, or if you were a rock or a human, or even an entirely different entity. There is an internal collection here specific to the individual soul. And it looks like it's a way to help you remember and grow in many ways.

S: Do you grow while you are in this resting place, or no?

J: You do grow, and it almost feels like a tree that leaves its rings throughout the middle. It's a level of ascension with each growth, with each movement up towards this beautiful divine floating light. We get closer and closer to it as we go through these lifetimes and these journeys. And it brings us back to this place so we may rest and feel this kind of encapsulation of ourselves within ourselves. In this place, we are reminded of who we really are. It helps to remind ourselves after we have had any existence, whether traumatic or any existence where we feel we have lost this connection. It helps us to connect back to our own individual place of experiences, whether these experiences are good or bad, or something that did not complete the way it was designed to be completed.

S: Do you find anything interesting about who you really are when you are there? Anything that stands out to you as interesting?

J: How big we really are! We are so much larger than our bodies on this planet. We are a lot of energy being pushed into a small human body, and that is very uncomfortable for many people.

S: How does that work exactly? How big are people?

J: The light, the energy that we really are looks huge. It could easily be larger than the size of your home. That is how large the orbit that we have is. And in the bodies that we have there is a lot of energy that does radiate out of us still. We have trouble containing it.

S: Tell me about that. We have trouble containing it in our bodies when we are here?

J: It looks like that is what our aura is, this bubble of energy around us that is our personal reflection. For each person it could be a different color as a reflection of their current state in this lifetime as they go towards whatever they set out to accomplish in this existence.

S: Is there anything that a person could do with their auras?

J: It would be helpful to know the color of your aura so that you could meditate on that color and feel what that means to you. If you feel specific colors coming across to you very strongly try to dwell afterwards on what that color means to you or represents in your life, what it links you to, what your accomplishments or goals are in this next phase of your life that you are in. Look and see if that is the color that suits who you truly are and try to take on the feeling of the other color that you would like to embrace, that you would like your energy to take on. Try to simplify it down into a feeling of color, because what comes across very strongly is that it is almost like an eternal mood ring that we underutilize greatly.

S: Do you see what your color is in this place?

J: Purple.

S: What does purple mean for you?

J: For Jen it means many things, but it also reminds her of how she has been stuck close to where Atlantis fell for all her incarnations after she died in Atlantis.

S: Why? Why is she stuck here?

J: This is something that she will finally change in this lifetime. She has been stuck here on the East Coast on purpose until she could finally recover and share this information.

S: Why did she have to stay close to where Atlantis was though?

J: The land you find yourself on has a great effect on you, and you feed off of it. The land that you are on in the physical world interacts with the energy that is trapped within your human body. And **it can continuously work against you or in favor of you based on how happy you are with your surroundings.**

S: You said that Jen will be able to move. What will happen if she does?

J: Moving will bring a new sense of understanding about herself and who she is. It will create that change of color and energy, and allow her to be in a different state. It's almost a whole different realm that you enter when you move. You can easily change this color to your energy. You can change the way it is charged; you can change the way it is emitted from you, how you feel about it, and how it affects others around you.

S: When you were in this room with the different levels, aside from noticing that you are very large, what else do you notice that seems interesting in that place?

J: While looking and feeling the energy throughout these levels there is a feeling of expansion that is very familiar, but also very exhilarating at the same time.

S: Tell me more.

J: This is what happens when we complete a level, the sphere that you really are, grows. The sphere that you are grows in power, energy, and mass. It grows more powerful.

S: What is that like?

J: That is what we essentially are at the end of the day. We are these giant spheres of energy that can form ourselves, and squish ourselves into these bodies or inanimate objects, or these different existences. But that is what we look like originally, and we grow, and we expand with it.

S: How do we squish ourselves into a little baby?

J: It's not that hard to do since it's energy, but it really looks squished in there, almost like a zipper being tugged in the back and zipped up all the way to the head to keep us in. I feel like it stays in, but for many it has these moments where it's too powerful and they feel this leaking or burst of this energy coming out. For some it can be very unhelpful in their current life because for many it may come off as a sign of mental instability. Many people with this type of leak don't understand all this energy coming out of them.

S: Tell me about that. What happens to these people?

J: From this perspective **it looks like a lot of mental illness can be truly understood in the afterlife as having too much energy put into one specific body, or a leak of it from some places on the body where it's not staying within and causing a change in the way that the person with this leak perceives things.** It's too much of a switch back and forth for them where they feel as if they can't consistently stay within this human body for the human experience. They go back and forth between this spherical all knowingness and the physical body. This causes too much instability for them in this current reality.

S: How does the leak happen? How can a person make their energy stay within them if they have this issue?

J: It is entirely up to the individual as they are planning their lives and looking through their other lives. Sometimes having this leak of energy is something they choose. But, for others it is something that will happen when they hit a point of uncomfortableness within this existence. They know that there is something happening within them, and they have to let that energy out somehow. This could possibly be the cause of schizophrenia or multiple personalities where a person isn't sure why they are switching between ways of being, or unsure of who they are, but it is just energy inside of them going ramped and not being able to deal with the confines of the body.

S: Is there anything a person can do if they believe this is happening to them?

J: Yes. By understanding this information, they can deeper understand themselves and why this is happening to them. It is important for them to understand that it isn't their fault that they have this unbound eternal energy that isn't a right fit for them. In many of these existences that people choose for themselves they sometimes come to the realization that their body isn't the right fit, but sometimes instead of ending the existence, they persist with their lifetime anyway and choose to deal with these issues. For some people this is the road that they have chosen to go down. It doesn't mean that they need to end the existence, it just means that they need to better understand what is happening to them. It can help a person's awakening to understand their eternal role in this greater project, experiment, that is never ending.

S: You said that you can look at history; can you tell me more about that?

J: On each of these rings, or levels, I can feel and see the lifetimes and people that I was. I feel the people I was connected to and the history of that time. It is a lot like a smart screen; it looks like something you would touch on this wall, but you don't really need to touch it at all, in order for it to give you the information of all of these lives.

S: Tell me more about this place? What else do you notice?

J: There is a very ancient energy here, with a very deep feeling of knowingness. It has the same energy as the Sphinx in Egypt. In fact, it is connected somehow. As I'm remembering this, I see that this energy has always existed. The history that is stored within the Sphinx goes back and back, and at one point goes all the way back to just being one. At one point everything was just one energy until it fractioned itself off and continued to divide, and divide, until we could all have these smaller experiences that we feel are individual, but we are actually just part of this larger collective. In the in-between we all come back to contribute to this collective that we are.

S: What is that like to give back to the collective?

J: It feels very fulfilling because you can't add anything wrong. Everything you have done, accomplished, and seen is greatly appreciated. No matter what you have done or failed to do while you are in a life.

S: In this resting place are you also aware of your future lives as well?

J: Only the next existence, but our future is dependent on what we are doing in this current life. We might not go to another lifetime here on Earth, we might go to other places or other Earths, but where we go next depends on where we are now. It depends on how that works out and what we are to accomplish in the next round. Many of us are moving into a new world.

CHAPTER 14: TWO CHOICES OF ASCENSION

There has been much confusion when it comes to the New Earth, ascension etc.... so I felt excited by the opportunity to have Jen answer questions while so deeply under hypnosis and within the resting place.

S: *Now that you are in that state where you can look around, connecting to the levels of the in-between, can you also connect with the information that is stored within the Sphinx?*

J: Yes, if I go through the levels I can connect. I'm connected now. I feel as if you can ask me questions while I'm here.

S: *Thank you! I would like to understand more about the new world and old world. Could you explain? Are we moving into a new world? Is this information within the Sphinx?*

J: Yes, the Sphinx is a communication device and it's connected to information. Let me see. Yes. This is a transitional time for many humans to move from the old world to the new world.

S: *Do we feel this difference?*

J: Yes, but it is a change in your physical world around you that is the deepest thing you will feel. There is a breaking down, a shattering of the old world.

S: *Will we notice this difference?*

J: Yes, it is within the mind and in the reflections of our minds that we create around us. It is as if you are tuning into something new; you're switching the channel to a new show. It may feel like that.

S: *I've had many clients say that this year they are leaving their bodies and moving onto a different Earth? Is this something that is actually happening?*

J: Yes, some people will ascend, and some have ascended already. These people are meant to leave their earthly bodies and begin work on a new world that is separate from this planet. Their spirits are traveling there to begin this work. It is not really their spirit; it is a mass of energy that will be needed to spark life in this new world. It isn't another planet or galaxy; it could be best described as a new world.

S: *Does everyone choose to go to the new world?*

J: No, not everyone has chosen that. Everyone chose and made their decisions before their incarnations. While you do have free will to alter things, you're not able to alter your decision to ascend to this separate new world or not.

S: *So, the people ascending to the new world made those decisions before they came in?*

J: Yes, because there is a very specific and detailed process required in beginning this new world. And the energy needed to begin this is being pulled from this Earth. That is why you see so many people ascending at the moment.

S: *What do you mean by we are seeing people ascend?*

J: A lot of people are passing. Some of them used the virus or the vaccine side effects as their exit point, and this acted like a guise to allow this ascension to happen for them. But **the virus itself is a very big trigger for the ascension, like a guise to allow this ascension to happen on this level.**

S: *What do you mean by that?*

J: This many people dying around the world without explanation to us on Earth would cause too much unsettlement and would affect the progress we still need to make on this planet. So, many people passing from this virus are going to this new world and they have chosen to leave their bodies and ascend during the time it is allowed for people to make a mass exit and begin this new world.

S: *Are all the people who are passing right now ascending?*

J: Not everyone, but many, and that was one of the purposes of the virus. The other purpose of the virus is to create within us the unsettling, the breaking down of what isn't working and the questioning that creates the new world here.

S: *Will Jen be leaving and ascending to this other new world?*

J: No, she will stay. This world will become a different type of world, and that is what she agreed to stay for. It will not remain the old world, it is just to show the separation during the ascension.

S: *Could you tell me more about that?*

J: Those who have humility will look to create something new on this Earth here.

S: *So, is there a new world and an old-world split?*

J: Yes, there are two choices that you were able to make when you planned this life. There are two choices of ascension. You may begin to ascend and begin the new world on this other planet that is being seeded, or you may stay and begin the new world here on Earth.

S: So, some people stay and begin the new world here, and some ascend and begin the new world there. What about the people that are full of negativity? I've heard that they leave with the old Earth. Is that true?

J: The growth of the new world depended on the negativity. The people full of negativity have been strategically placed in your lives to create for you the questioning that allows humans to move away from things they don't want and to create new what they do want. The negativity has served a purpose and without it there would not be growth on either new world. The negativity is not a result of the individual that you would describe as negative. They are in fact playing a specific role and the negativity is actually the energy that has been thrown from the universe to be expelled by these individuals for these specific reasons.

S: What about people who do not choose to ascend to either of these new Earths?

J: Some have chosen not to ascend within this lifetime, and for many it is only with the understanding that they, when they choose to incarnate again, will incarnate into the new world. There are some that need to see the old world through to the end of its death. They have been sworn, like almost taking an oath, to see through it to the end. And they will do so, and they will usher it out. And that will make many people uncomfortable, but it is their role. And it is ok to let them do that.

S: How do people ascend to the new world? I've heard clients talking about natural disasters that may usher this in.

J: Yes, there are many ways to ascend and that will be another way, but the natural disasters will signify the beginning of a new Earth here. The natural disasters will have no effect on the new world beyond us though.

S: Why is there a new world away from this one?

J: There is always a need for a backup planet in case of the unthinkable happening, but also the need for this new world is part of an evolutionary step for us. It is us coming back full circle to the home planet. The new world that we are seeding, that some are ascending to now, is the original home planet for many. We left that planet to come here only to go back to it.

S: So, we left what some call the new world only to come back to it? Why?

J: To allow it time to regenerate during the time we spent away, almost as if this Earth is our summer home. This is a natural progression that we go through when we inhabit planets. We inhabit them until they are done with their life cycle, then we inhabit a different planet. We are constantly moving from planet to planet and constantly evolving.

S: Are we all from that home planet?

J: Not all, but most of us have mixed blood that goes back to this planet. Most of us.

S: So, this world that some are ascending to isn't really a new world, it's just a place where most of us used to live. We just gave it time to regenerate.

J: It will be new when it is being created. The mission was to go back at a certain point in our development when we were mentally ready to rebuild and to reconstruct our beloved planet. **It hurts people to know that they could not be a part of this planet, that they had to leave. Many just want to go back home.**

S: Many want to just go back home?

J: Many do. It is in our cells, our blood, it's in every bit of our essence to want to go home. But we knew it would take a while, a lot of time. **And from the beginning, that has been the experiment, to create a place, Earth, where we could be, and where we could wait for our beloved home to be ready**. But so much has happened since then, so much has gone wrong. So much has been altered in the planning of this planet Earth that this is a moment of reckoning that allows us to begin our journey back.

S: Can you tell me more about the home planet, or the new world?

J: There are these pyramids with spires on the new world that are banks of information that were left there purposely. They are the communication devices, and we can connect with these devices through the Sphinx.

S: Tell me more about that.

J: Yes. There are pyramids with spires at the top that stick up straight then create like a curlicue curling up into the sky. There are many of them there, and these hold all of our history. The history of that planet and all of our history on this planet as well. They were made in the same way the Sphinx was made, as a time capsule, record keeper, a beacon, and a communication device.

S: Is there anything within this information that you notice that seems important?

J: There is so much, but importantly this device shows how it was our destiny to come back to this planet. But the planet needed time; it needed to die. It needed to be brought back into a different dimensional vibration.

S: Why?

J: **Because the physical realm of that home planet had no nutrient left to support life. We needed to ascend into a different form so that we could eventually return back home and match that vibrational frequency that the planet is now created of. The home planet/ new world itself has ascended because it could no longer support life. As we ourselves left that planet in physical form and came to Earth, the goal has always been to evolve to where we could return back to our home in whatever condition home is in now.**

S: What is the condition now?

J: The condition home is in now is like a cosmic energy where our bodies need to be almost spirit-like to be there. It's very hard to explain because this wouldn't make sense here on Earth and there aren't any words to describe it. The English language does not even come close to having the words I would need to translate this and the closest thing I can find to describe this is that the planet is just an energy replica of a planet.

S: *Will there be a time when we all move back to this old/new world?*

J: Some will; many will. Some will also choose to move on to the next adventure, to something even newer, and that would be the continuation of this great journey.

S: *Could you tell me more about the new world on this Earth?*

J: The most probable timelines show that the population will drop. There will be a lowered percentage of children being born and some opportunities for chaos for this time of transitioning. But once this chaos is over, and this ascension has taken place, we can begin the truth within the new world here on this Earth, then we will rebalance. We will rebalance as a population over time to a less alarming rate of growth that will be naturally more sustainable. It will allow us to create a homeostasis for the way we will begin to create our future on this planet.

S: *What is the future like for this planet?*

J: More communities will be built that will not guide by religion or culture, or even a specific language, but in regard to very sustainable living. Things will be harnessed from the Earth in a beneficial manner like the sun, wind and even UV lights. And there will be lots of advancements being made. The future on this Earth will be a great time for equality and growth.

S: *When do you see that happening?*

J: This is all happening now.

CHAPTER 15: EXTRA-TERRESTRIAL (ET) CONTACTS

As Jen was recounting her experience and memories in the in-between state, I was curious to know more about her extra-terrestrial contacts.

S: Could you tell me more about your ET contacts?

J: There is a similarity in the likeness of the dimensional being that I once was as an ET Commander on a different planet and the beings that would come and form these upkeep checks, but we are not the same entity or energy port.

S: Have you as the Commander ever taken anyone, or made contact in that way?

J: No.

S: What is it like for the beings that do contact and take people?

J: It is very professional and well organized. There is a circuit that they travel on. They go from different organized planet colonies to the next, visiting the different children and adults that have been planted there.

S: Do they feel anything when they contact these people?

J: They feel a different sense of love and gratitude for the sacrifice that the humans are making while being here on Earth and preforming these tasks. But there is not a feeling of pity or anything like that for them. It is a different kind of feeling; it's an understanding on the level of preorganized contracts that have been organized and arranged. They are just doing their job.

S: Is there any emotion involved when they do these upkeeps?

J: They are tapped into who they really are, why they are here, and their understanding of where we originally come from, and go back to, is very strong. So, there is not a sense of ambiguous understanding of what they're doing. There is a tight nit dependency between the extra-terrestrial and the human during these contacts.

S: How do they feel about who they are? What do they know?

J: They have an extension of a divine consciousness within them. They are still tapped into this string that pulls them back to the eternal source that we all come from. We, as humans are very detached from this here on Earth, but they are still able to maintain this contact. So, they operate on that level of this higher intelligence and higher consciousness that doesn't need to feel the things that we feel.

S: *What does it feel like to still be attached to this all-knowing consciousness?*

J: It feels very much like there is a white type of energy that flows into you and keeps you very energized and very full of joyous movement. Everything that you do is done in this very confident and professional manner.

S: *How would you describe where the Commander is now?*

J: A part of me as the Commander rests within the genetic code and within that same cylindrical hallway of records that you would go to in the in-between, and a part of me is who you call Jen. But I as the Commander am also the one talking to you now.

S: *Is there anything else that you could tell me about the new world?*

J: We have been trying to colonize the new world since before we started the first colonies here on Earth. It is a very mass orchestrated event to continue this now; there are many beings from all over the Universe who are helping.

S: *Could you tell me about that?*

J: Because of the fear virus on this planet, we needed to wait until the frequency was at a certain level and we are hitting that level now. The new world is still very new, fresh, and young and just like a baby being born, **but there's just not a lot of people there**. It's very slow and will take some time for people to inhabit it.

S: *Are the hybrid children there?*

J: The hybrid children are there, but the new people coming are very slow to come.

S: *When you say the new people coming, do you mean the people leaving this Earth to go there?*

J: Yes. They are those who are ascending and who are not staying on this Earth. Some have chosen to stay here, to complete whatever is needed, and others are completing by ascending and they are ascending to the new world.

S: *Do people have to die to ascend to the new world?*

J: No, and there is truly no such thing as death. However, there is no need for the physical body in going to the new world. So, the removal of the self from the physical body seems to be the way forward.

S: When do you see that happening?

J: It is happening. It's just not happening very fast; there is a very slow trickle at the moment. There still is something that needs to be done to open the faucet.

S: Could you tell me about that?

J: I don't see too much about this for some reason.

S: What about the hybrid children? What is their purpose?

J: They are there to help guide us once we get there. We have created these familiar beings in order to guide, to lead, and to instruct, but in a very nurturing way. They will teach us how to be in the new world, how to be happy, and how to be a part of this new place. They are to be guides for people, essentially, they are in charge. They are to be the guardians and the keepers of the new world as they grow and continue the work that they are meant to do.

S: How does a human know if they have hybrid children?

J: There are many who will feel that they have had a fantom pregnancy, or that they have had a visitation with a being, and have had parts of their body, perhaps parts of their reproductive systems taken from them in some ways. And they will not understand this. This is something I feel many people repress, and push down deep away, and assume it was something they have just maybe seen in a movie and don't remember or could not understand. But there is a very deep feeling of loss that something was taken from them for some of these people. Something was done to them, and they can't understand what it was. Sometimes they may feel this loss of a child, especially for many women and most of the time it doesn't make sense, but they still have a nagging feeling that there was something that was taken from them.

S: Where do these children go exactly?

J: They are taken to…what I can see from my own…it's like a spherical circular room. A room with no corners to it and a domed ceiling that has light that emanates from it. It isn't one single light source. And around the room they have many tubes that the children are held in. It looks like artificial wombs, but they are very large. And they will keep these hybrids in there for quite some time, until they are a bit older. They stay in the artificial wombs for about ten to twelve months. It is longer than the gestation period inside a human body.

S: Why do they stay there for so long?

J: It looks like these hybrids need extra time within these artificial wombs because they won't have the closeness of a mother or a human body for sustenance or to meet their needs after they are created.

S: I have heard that these mothers visit these children? Is that correct?

J: Yes. They bring the mothers to their hybrid children when these mothers are asleep. It's like a dimensional trip where you can still be within your body sleeping in your bed, but they can ascend a part of you to visit with the children and to see them. But it is not the same feeling as one would feel with their children here on Earth. There is a bit of a disconnect because you see them and they are hybrids, they are you and someone else…and you do not know who that someone else is. And you don't have the attachment of a long pregnancy or the strain on the body that attaches one to it, nor the bonding and connection after the birth. So, there is a disconnect that takes place for those who do go to view their hybrid children and that's why not all of the mothers are allowed to go, and rarely are you allowed to remember any of these things because it is too traumatic and taxing on the human mind for some people to understand and comprehend this.

S: The purpose for these hybrid children is to be guides for the new world?

J: They are the keepers, the guides, the officiants. They are the orchestrators within. In some cases, the mothers give birth to these hybrids with the intention that the mother will incarnate into that body when she arrives in the new world.

S: Tell me more.

J: This is an option for those who have chosen to volunteer for this program as hosts for these hybrids.

S: What are these children like?

J: They are very free spirited and open in understanding. They are very intelligent; they are very ethereal. They have this beautiful presence to them. The best way to describe it would be to call it Zen. You feel this need to be in their presence. There is safety in their presence, and a calmness to them.

S: Why couldn't some other being be there to be guides in the new world? Why is there this hybridization program?

J: **The other beings are not something that you would look at and say this is us, and this is our new world. We would feel like visitors. When there is a part of you that you are rejoining and growing onto, then it is, and feels, like YOUR new world.**

S: Is that the only reason for the hybridization program or is there another reason?

J: That is reason for the hybridization program that I work with, but there are many hybridization programs. We are definitely not alone in this massiveness that we are in. Even though many of you relate back to your ancestors coming to this planet, they are not the only ones out there.

S: I've had other women, especially post-menopausal women, come in for a session because they feel pregnant, and they don't know what is happening to them. They know what a pregnancy feels like and when their doctors claim that there isn't anything wrong, and nothing shows up on the medical scans, they have nowhere to turn for answers. I've had quite a few come in for a session and their higher selves have claimed just what you said, that they are indeed pregnant and seeding the new world. Is there anything else that you could tell me about this?

J: It is common and something that was agreed upon before their incarnation here. The older women are having a pregnancy that is easier to hide and less traumatic. The position of hosting these children through pregnancies is a highly coveted service and not all can do this. We are careful with who is allowed to do this to keep the new world pure. It is not a position that just anyone can have.

Below is a session which illustrates this phenomenon. Even though I'm only including one, I had four women come with the same issues between August 2020 and April 2021.

Amelia came in for a session because she was a sixty-one-year-old post-menopausal woman who had been to several doctors trying to find out why she had a strong feeling that she was pregnant. In each doctor's office no sign of a fetus was discovered on any scan, and no one could find anything wrong. Amelia was prescribed Ativan for her anxiety and told that she could not possibly be pregnant. When talking to her beforehand she claimed that had wanted to have a QHHT session because she knew that something was happening. She had given birth to three healthy baby girls in her lifetime, and she explained that she knew what a pregnancy felt like. This is her session:

S: *What do you notice?*

A: I see a being looking over me. I'm inside a ship right now.

S: *Tell me more.*

A: I'm on a table, it feels cold but I'm comfortable. There's a bright light and what looks like a lot of medical equipment near the lights.

S: *What do you notice if you focus on yourself?*

A: I'm very calm, but they are putting something inside of me. They are going into my vagina and putting something in there.

S: *Tell me more.*

A: This has happened before. I feel good about this though for some reason.

S: *You feel good about it?*

A: Yes, I see that I'm part of a hybridization program. I've volunteered to help seed a different place. This is going to sound really crazy. Maybe I'm making this up!

S: *You're doing great, keep going, what do you notice?*

A: This is really crazy, but I used to be the one doing these experiments! I've just signed up to be the one experimented on this time! I'm carrying a baby that is part me, part them.

S: How would you describe the people doing this to you?

A: They are extra-terrestrials, but really, we are them in a way, they are our ancestors.

S: Why do they need to put a baby inside of you?

A: Because they can't have natural births anymore. So, they need to use humans to create new people to seed a new place is what I'm being told. So, these new children will be hybrids which are a combination of these aliens and humans.

S: Why can't they reproduce any longer?

A: Because they advanced too far into their technology and abandoned their emotional bodies. So, they need our creative spark. They want to be able to redo this and develop differently now that they see what happened when they only advanced with their technology. They wish they had kept doing things in a more natural way and by creating new beings for themselves to inhabit they can do this over. I'm not crazy, this is really happening. And it's not scary! I signed up for this. Wow. This is happening to multiple women as well. I just realized something though.

S: What do you notice?

A: I actually see that I am not just the one on the table, but also the one doing this experiment!!! I am both, and the person talking to me is also me. Wow, I feel so much peace and understanding now. This all makes sense.

CHAPTER 16: THE PROCESS OF ASCENSION

As Jen recounted her memories of the in-between place, we learned interesting information about the Ascension.

S: Is there anything else that you notice in this in-between place that seems interesting?

J: We must not go backwards. We must continue to move forward into this.

S: Move forward into what exactly?

J: We are destined to move into a kinder, gentler Earth. And I know that sounds foolish, but it's a place we are moving towards, where we just do not live the same way that we have been living, through ego and greed. People are becoming more understanding, nurturing, caring, tolerant and openminded. We are just expanding our consciousness in such ways that we should not move backwards. We should move forward into this.

S: How are we moving forward? Can you tell me more?

J: There is a tremendous energy that is projected down on the Earth right now. It looks from this perspective almost like a whiteish blue light that kind of bubbles around the Earth. It is changing us. We are changing drastically, and some are ascending. Some are going to the new world, some are staying, but we are definitely not staying the same. We are recreating, transforming what our lives are here. Few people are happy in the lives that they have had here. People have had so little say in these lives.

S: Tell me more about this energy hitting the Earth?

J: It is like a whitish blue bubble that seems to surround the Earth.

S: Where does it come from?

J: It is brought down to us like a natural energy that is attracted to Earth that has surrounded us. We have pulled this towards us because we are ready for this type of movement, this change, this ascension.

S: Where does this whitish blue light come from originally?

J: It is very hard to give that a name. It is truly just pulled in from the Universe. It is the same pull that brings us anything or does anything in this Universe. It is the same energy that conspires to bring us what we need.

S: So, do you mean that it can help with manifestation?

J: It can, but what you wish to manifest has to truly serve you. You are bigger than just your conscious deciding because you are in so many different places at once and on so many different levels. You can't in this conscious body truly connect with all of those pieces to fully understand if something isn't serving you, so it can easily become disappointing for humans to use this if they do not understand the full picture of why they are not getting what they have asked for. Sometimes it will not serve them in the grand scheme of what they are here to accomplish.

S: But if it does serve them, they will get what they want?

J: If it is something that will serve them, and they are a match to it, then yes. But if it is just wanting and needing and not something that ultimately serves them, then it would be harder.

S: Ok. So, this energy will change humans no matter what they do? Is that correct?

J: Yes.

S: Are humans feeling anything as this energy surrounds the planet?

J: Many can feel a difference. Many can feel that their lives are very different than they were a few months ago. And they can feel this energy in their lives. They can feel a newness about them, almost as if at some point in the last few months they saw the world animated for the first time in their lives. They saw it light up. They felt this energy and they felt this new life force that was around them here. This new way of looking at things. This new feeling of... almost like an optimism for the future. It feels like a clearing has taken place for many. That is a lot of what they feel from this energy.

S: Could you tell me more about the purpose of this energy?

J: It is mostly used to clear us, to remove the parts of us that are not serving us, the parts of us that are stuck within our ego. There are parts of us that we have been lied to about.

S: Could you tell me more about that?

J: There are so many things that we have been told we need to possess or accomplish. Or the unnecessary roles that we are told that we need to provide in other's lives. These are all just things that have been told to us that are not truths.

S: And those are being cleared?

J: Yes, they are being cleared for many. They are being lifted, removed, almost like they are being pulled from these people in these long lines of energy that moves into this blue bubble that is being pulled away from them. And some want to go with this energy. Some leave their bodies and go with it; others remain in these bodies here but are clear. There is this clearing that is happening.

S: When a person leaves their body and goes with this energy line, where exactly do they go?

J: It is different than the physical body leaving; the physical body on Earth just does not seem to leave Earth. You cannot take the physical body with you, but the physical body is actually very unimportant. It's really nothing, it's like a costume, an outer machine. The important part of you leaves and then there is an opportunity for another being to take your place if that is what you have both agreed. If another being takes your place than it would not have to experience a childhood and could finish this life out for you. Some call this a walk-in.

S: Where does the part of you that leaves go?

J: At first it just lifts up and goes into this blue energy, then it looks like this bright light happens and it just shoots off far away. It looks like a beautiful shooting star shooting across the Universe, all in the same direction. It looks like most are going to the new world when this happens. It looks like a dimensional hop, where it is just this bright light that shoots off and then dissipates and you don't see it anymore. But it doesn't disappear, it doesn't go away, it just goes into something else, this new dimension, this new place. It doesn't need to go far. It's almost like it's right there. But to get into it, to break through that barrier you almost become this bright white light as you travel fast and shoot right into this other dimension, into the new world.

S: What happens when you break through that barrier?

J: There is an immense relief, an overwhelming feeling of euphoria and breaking away of everything. There is immediate understanding of who you truly are and who you were. This remembrance happens instantly.

S: What do people remember when this happens?

J: That we are all just these eternal beings that are hell bent on having experience.

S: Why exactly?

J: Because if there is no experience, then there is nothing. And experience is what we are looking for.

S: How long will this energy be surrounding the planet?

J: A good couple of years, it looks like five years.

S: Why now? Why is this energy surrounding us now?

J: This is the first time we have started to reach a level of understanding within ourselves, that this is something we were supposed to do. We have just had way too many years of repression, of being told that enlightening ourselves was wrong, stupid, foolish, or crazy. And people have pulled away from it and did not want to embrace it. But we have in so many ways lost that stigma now, and people have decided to delve in, even with any lingering stigma, forgoing the opinions of others.

S: What have we forgotten that we wanted to accomplish?

J: What we forget upon our arrival are these life goals that we have planted and designed for ourselves, before our existences. But we remember these things upon our journey into the next dimension because part of our goal was to be able to accelerate into that new dimension and to ascend, to leave. And that is why those who are going feel that they are going. This is the next leg of their journey. While I can't give you a finite answer of what they will do there and why they would go there, I know the answer is experience and it will continuously be experience. Because we will never ever be able to experience everything. And that is the only thing that keeps this continuum going. It's the knowledge that we can try as hard as we'd like, but having experience is what keeps us going, that is why energy cannot die, it cannot be killed. If you do not have experience, you are constantly bored, you are stuck, you are stagnant. Experience is the opposite of that stagnation; anything is better than stagnation. Even in the worst of an existence, the experience is greater than the stagnation.

S: Tell me more.

J: There is a need to continuously keep your energy active, to keep your energy fluid and moving and growing. And the energy itself changes over time. It evolves and that is the ultimate goal of all of this activity, of all of this movement. It is the evolvement of this eternal energy inside of you.

S: So, the energy inside of you is evolving?

J: Yes, it is your spirit, this eternal energy that we are, your eternal beingness that continuously evolves. The purpose is to continuously add onto it, to evolve it, and to grow.

S: I've had some clients tell me that they're going through a really hard time. They feel very emotional. What is happening?

J: It is the venting of what looks like tens of thousands of years of regression being lifted off of the souls of people. While they are starting to see things differently, they're going through tumultuous times in order to shed, to pull off, to release themselves from this repression. It can't just be done from a joyous standpoint of conscious decision. It's not meant to be comfortable; it's not meant to put you at ease in the beginning of the process.

S: Are people clearing other's trauma as well as their own?

J: There are so many levels of trauma for so many, that are being lifted. Trauma from their past, trauma from their genetic past, trauma from their present.

S: Aside from just letting this happen is there any advice for humans?

J: Just continue to go through the process, find a way to be ok with what happens. And it will be miraculous what will happen to people when they begin to allow this, to bravely look into their future and remove these burdens that they have cast upon themselves through these existences.

S: What will happen after a person goes through this?

J: They will feel this relief. It's not something that will happen in a day; this can take a long time. **I have to tell you Sarah, I feel Dolores around. She seems very happy!**

S: She does? Why does she seem happy?

J: She is excited to watch us and is helping as much as she can. She is happy to watch the continuation of this work, and happy to know how involved she has been throughout this process, and that she was able to guide this to where it is.

S: So, she is the one guiding us?

J: She is. She is here, but there are things that she can't do, even though she can be a guiding force. We were the completion of her work that was revealed to her after she passed away, and she continues to help us, but other things have to happen in our lives to allow this information to unfold. While she is watching and is involved, she is not the one who is allowed to intervene in some areas.

S: Was there anything else that she noticed upon her passing away that she wished she could convey to the world?

J: She understood right away that we would be the ones to share this information and that this information had to wait for the right time, and that this is the right time. She sees how humanity is waking up and what the pandemic has done for all of us. This was something that was alluded to her, and something that she touches upon in her work, but she was not given the full picture then, and it was not something that would have helped had it been released beforehand.

S: Sometimes I feel as if she is leading every step of my journey; is she?

J: She is. In many ways she's guiding it, she is part of it, because she is a part of this! But we have also made these decisions before our lifetimes as to how this would come out and when it would come out. And it was something that she had forgotten during her lifetime and now has remembered as she is in the afterlife, the in-between. It is a little bit like knowing, not knowing, then knowing again. And knowing better than to do too much intervention. But guiding is very different from intervening. She knows her role is to guide, and she follows through. And she watches what happens. But she is also in many other places at once where she is helping to release other bits of information through others. We are not the only ones who are given information, but we have been given very special information, a stimulus, something meant to provoke thought. And others are being given information that will eventually add on to the next level of this. It may not necessarily be connected to our work, but it will all fit into a larger picture.

S: Thank you!

CHAPTER 17: CONTROL OVER HUMANS

As I looked further into our history with Jen the theme of control and power was often brought up. Here is a more in-depth look at this power struggle for control that we as humans have had to account for.

J: It's interesting as I look through these walls of this resting place how there has been so much control over humans.

S: *Why do humans want control over one another?*

J: It is something we brought with us to this planet. As I search through our history and go further and further back to see why we would do that, it brings me back to the fear virus.

S: *Why would we do this? On other planets, isn't it usually blissful?*

J: Not all planets. There are others that have their issues, there are some that are probably in a way worse off situation than us.

S: *Can you tell me about one of those planets that is in a worse situation?*

J: There are some that are not doing as well as we are. Whether these are planets, parallel Universes, dimensions, or focusing points of energy, there are so many other places where other beings exist that have parallel understandings to the world that we are in. There are many options as to where you can go, and when we choose, we create alternate possibilities and realities. We have to understand our multidimensional nature. There really are parts of us here, and parts of us out there, that are on other colonies that we have set up throughout the Universe. We are not the only colony or the only planet, and there are other colonies and planets that have had disastrous results. Some of them have just been abandoned, others have just done themselves in so many times that they refuse to restart their experiment and have just let themselves die. Some planets have just been left cold and bare.

S: *I just had a client who while regressed under hypnosis found herself on a different planet where her job was to build moons that would allow for the planet to have energy. It was wonderful until it became too much energy for the planet and the planet finally died. The higher self said that this planet was called Jupiter. Do you see this as well?*

J: Yes. However, the other colonizing planets that I was talking about are far away from here. We are very isolated in our experiment on this planet. And if that work was done on Jupiter, it was done before Earth's planet was habitable and producing humans. But again, this is dimensional in some ways so there could be an overlap.

S: Why are we so isolated?

J: Because when we seeded Earth, we were looking for a very unique outcome to come from this isolation. If we did not know as humans that there were others out there like us, how would we behave? What would happen to us if we were to eventually find out? There are so many things that come into play with this isolation that it becomes a very unique variable in this experiment.

S: Why haven't we been told the truth about extraterrestrials?

J: Because there is a very strong element of control that guides and guards this. The governing fear of losing work force is too much to risk for countries that have production quotas and things that need to be done and met. There was too much money and power hinging on our ignorance and complacency. We are programed to keep working and we are kept busy. When we know that there are other races out within other Universes, it can allow for the mind to question and possibly think in a very different way. And that is very dangerous for people who make money off of those who don't have to think very hard. It all comes down to money and the loss of money. But there is a great effort to help us move through this transition and ascension. Some of us will stay because we know it is our mission and our duty to see this through to the end, but others will know that it is fine to go, and it is time to transition and go to what this has always been meant to be, this idyllic place that no longer has the fear virus destroying us and turning us against each other.

S: Why do we need to leave this fear behind?

J: Because we are meant to meet with these other planets eventually, who do not have this virus. We're meant to meet at an evolutionary point when we remove this fear virus. And some places have the fear virus as well; other places don't; other places have other things that we can't even begin to understand that have impeded them. This is not unique within us to be the ones who are messed up and not working right. This is a very big experiment. And there are so many variables to it. We are special in this experiment though because we are so isolated.

S: Tell me more about the resting place. What else do you notice there?

J: You can connect to anything you would like. Some people will sit and float and look and try to understand all of it. But when you connect to the information within the Sphinx, you realize that everything that has ever been done and all of our experiences were for one reason, and that reason was just to get us here.

S: So, everything was leading to this moment?

J: Yes. Everything is leading to this evolution, to this journey of being able to transport yourself out of this body and using your mind to be able to transfer yourself to a new place, to a place where we have been trying to get to for so long. We have had to build through our trials and tribulations and our upsets and our happiness. All of this has helped to build this new place. And we leave our fear here. **We could not go to the new world with fear, but over the last year, almost all of us have lost a lot of that fear.** We have given it up, we have said we do not need you; you do not serve us.

S: Could you tell me more about the future of this Earth?

J: This planet will be scrubbed and cleaned and put back in its rightful place.

S: What about the humans on this planet?

J: They are meant to inherit an enjoyable Earth until a time when this experiment ends.

S: How long will that take?

J: There is still a very long time ahead, perhaps another million years before we get to that point.

S: What about the future of the new world? What is that future like?

J: It is very idyllic, relaxing, and promising. It doesn't have this tense bitterness to it that kind of makes you wonder what is going to happen. You feel very confident there knowing it's ok; it is what we wanted it to be. This new world is what we have tried to create, and we've been successful. We have taken all the good that we have looked for, but we are not making it so that it is just this planet where nothing bad ever happens. That is not the point. It is still to be a place of experience and of things that need to change over time. And with that we will have our ups and our downs. But in this new place we will see how we do without this anxiety, this element of fear constantly pushing us in the wrong directions and pushing us against each other. When we communicate and work together, and when we are compassionate with each other, it feels good.

S: With all this energy on the planet helping us, is it also changing the people you would call corrupt as well?

J: It is exposing them. It is less about changing them and more about exposing them and taking away from them the gratification of getting away with things. We cannot continuously enable a system that applauds corruption and secretly looks to be the corruptor.

S: Is there anything else about the other planets that look interesting?

J: One that I see is smaller than Earth, about half the size of Earth. It looks like it has a lot more water and more of a mountainous strip of land throughout the water. The inhabitants seem very calm and wide-eyed, and they have a grayish tone to their skin. Their noses are not like ours; their noses look like two smaller holes. They don't need this longer nose that we have, and they don't have ears like us either. On this planet they are able to communicate telepathically.

S: How are they advancing? Where are they on their evolutionary path?

J: They are on a different mission than us and that is why they have a smaller planet. They have more control in some ways.

S: *Tell me about that.*

J: This planet is less messed up than we are. It has been more of a perfect example of an experiment than Earth was.

S: *The only thing that messed up the Earth experiment was the fear virus. Correct?*

J: Yes.

S: *Are there any surprising benefits of the fear virus?*

J: It has given us a different path and while not all would see it as beneficial, it has brought us to where we are.

S: *I've heard many beings want to come to Earth because it's harder. Is this because of the fear virus or has it always been like that?*

J: It has always been like that, but the fear virus has added an extra element to this that has brought more attraction to this planet. People are looking for experience. What I'm seeing on that other smaller planet is that it's actually kind of boring there. This is one of the conclusions that has been drawn, that without this constant shakeup and everyday drama within life, that life can be very boring. There isn't much to be gained within this constant state of perfection. The true knowledge and true gaining that we are able to obtain through our lifetimes, especially here on this Earth, comes from the diversity that we experience through problems and conflict. This is one of the reasons why many come here.

S: *Are there any other planets that are more difficult than this one?*

J: I'm sure there are, but I can't see one right now.

S: *Do you appreciate the difficult times when you get to the other side? Do you appreciate the sad times? What do you do with all your collective experiences?*

J: What you have lived through becomes almost like a badge of honor, and it allows you to move forward in evolvement as an eternal being. For eternity you will have these constant changes happening in these different lifetimes. Change creates new growth, new identity, and a new everything for you to learn from and to grow from. And this transforms you into the next level and it never ends. It is an undying, unending experience.

S: *When the civilizations of Atlantis and Lemuria were destroyed, all those souls met in the afterlife, and they chose to come back now. Why now?*

J: We have tried before this time to redo this; this isn't the first time after those cataclysms that we have come together and said, let us try. There were at least a half dozen attempts at different points in time, where we have failed, and civilizations once again were destroyed. But the point we are at right now is very unique in comparison to where we have been before. We have the technology on our side this time and the ability to communicate with each other very quickly and are able to spread ideas and information faster, and that is one of the unique things that we have been able to regain in this lifetime in comparison to that lifetime in Atlantis and Lemuria. This time we are once again in tune with our crystals. We are more in tune with the energy it brings. We carry devices with us all the time that have crystals inside of them that allow us to communicate on an entirely different level with each other.

S: Do you mean with cell phones?

J: Yes, computers as well. All of these things are powered with small crystals within them. This is the closest lifetime we have come to as far as technology, in comparison to that lifetime in Atlantis. There has never been a time like this in most recent history where information and access to information was so readily available, to help humans awaken. The light from the tablets, phones, devices are creating changes to the human brain as well. It is rewiring the brain so that humans are becoming used to and learning instant manifestation. It is lighting up areas of the brain that have never been lit up before and it's creating a coordination in the synapses that is creating an enlightening effect.

S: So, there is a hidden benefit to the cell phone?

J: Yes.

S: What about radiation and exposure?

J: Of course, there is a balance one should keep, and a knowing when one has had too much exposure. But there is an adaptation process occurring in humans, as there was in ancient man with the radiation that was in bananas. The small amounts of radiation then, and now, lead to more growth and expansion in the human brain that would never have happened without the radiation. However, when you come into a world with the disease of fear often times things that could have a beneficial component to them could also become misconstrued as being completely dangerous. There is always a benefit to everything within this Universe.

S: Could you tell me more about the different timelines and existences?

J: It looks like each individual has their own bubble of reality, but we fail to see that many of the bubbles around us are actually us living in other existences and other bodies as well at the same time. We are not only within one, but we are within many, and we can cross through the boundaries of time because time is very irrelevant and very insincere. There really isn't this natural border that we think there is.

S: What do you mean by that?

J: Time itself is fake. It is an invention to help organize people and control people. It was created in order to get things done, in order for people to run efficiently, and in order for money to be made or goods to be traded. But the truth is that you can be living within different centuries all at the same time and also interact as yourself on this level too.

S: Can you tell me more about that?

J: It's very similar to how you would be in several different bodies on this planet at the same time in many different incarnations. There is a bigger purpose and goal in living in all of these places at once and doing all of this at once. There is a grand prize that you really do receive by doing this.

S: So, after you go through the levels in the in-between, what happens next?

J: You wake up, look around, and you feel that you are done with your resting. And you feel that you are done with looking at your other lives, that you are ready to look, with the help of your guide, through your recent existence. This is so that you can fully see your most recent past life for what it was, and fully see what opportunities you took, and what opportunities you missed. You see how your life changed, ebbed, and flowed through the choices you made and how it matched up to this eternal understanding of what had you mapped out for yourself. And you have this part of you there, with you, as you remind yourself of what your goals were as you go through it all. But this guide is really just you, another version of you that is there with you. It's just a version of you that has not forgotten, one that has not had to go into this physical body and forget. Because when you enter into the physical body you forget everything until you come back here and remember. But this part of you that never forgets is somewhere above you always, and always remembers who you are, and is who ultimately brings you back together at the end of this.

S: What does this part of you on the other side do during your life? Does it help you? Guide you?

J: Yes, it sends you signs, and that is where the signs come from most of the time. There is so much that you are constantly telling yourself about what you have planned for yourself, that you are constantly trying to remind yourself about. It is all you, but just different levels of you that has this memory and never had to take on the burden of a human body and the forgetting that goes with it. **Many call this part of you the higher self. It is exactly what you contact in a QHHT session.**

S: So, you meet up with this part of you there, and it goes over your life with you?

J: Yes, there is a part of us that we keep, almost like a time capsule, far away from this human life and body so that it won't be tainted by what we must become to be here, to gain this experience in a human body.

S: When you go about reviewing your life as Christie, were there any opportunities that you noticed that you missed, that you were surprised about?

J: I see that there was a very early opportunity for my mom to marry a different man who wouldn't have been so terrible to us. I see the missed opportunity there; it is one of the first things I see. I knew that I was going to be born to her, and I knew that I was going to be born to a single mother at a time where it was very unacceptable, and I understood that going into this life. But I knew that my mother and her decision making would have a large role in how I would be shaped throughout this life. And while receiving and reviewing this information I see how she chose someone who she thought would be a better provider for us, rather than someone who truly would've loved us.

S: What about for you? Do you notice any opportunities that you missed?

J: I see the opportunity I had to not tell my coworkers about what I had uncovered, and the life that follows could have been fulfilling in many ways. But also, if I had ignored that understanding of what I uncovered with Julie, then I would have repressed it down inside and I would've had to again repeat that in this life.

S: So, every time you make a different choice there is a different outcome? You have said before that there is a different version of yourself whenever you make a lifechanging decision.

J: Yes. There are many bubbles of myself that have lived many separate lives, in many different ways, and they are all gaining valuable experience. But it doesn't take away from this being the most important life, that the one I'm in now and the one I was in then are the most important ones. Experiences that splinter off and become their own separate realities and own separate versions of what happened are real, but they are fractions from the original and not the original themselves.

S: So, if you hadn't shared that information until you digested and understood it, then you wouldn't have had to repeat this?

J: Yes, it looks like that version or potential for that life was very fulfilling had I shared this information at the right time. But still there was a potential for it to not work and even for the potential to suppress all that information which would've led to a very mundane life and a life of regret later. I would have felt regret that I did not do more with the information that I was given at that age.

S: When you planned this life as Jen, what did you notice?

J: I'm very excited to have a family this time. I know I'm not going to be by myself in this life, and I chose parents who will not trade me in for something better. This time I chose parents who will stick by me. I have a solid foundation to uncover this information from. I will be given more of an opportunity, and I will be in a different world where I will not have the same restrictions that will be held against me this time. It looks freer and happier; it looks more enjoyable. I feel that I'm excited to start this life as Jen in the same place too, I will start this life in NYC in the same area. It is comforting.

S: Do you see anything interesting about your current life?

J: I see where other things were chosen at different points that have led me here.

S: Any missed opportunities that you notice?

J: I see that I have delayed this by my own choosing, that this could have happened earlier. But I chose at one point to delay this for what looks like about eight years. I don't think I was ready for this yet, and I understood that at the time, and did not want to risk having the same reaction and lack of understanding as I did in my past existence. I needed to have more trust in myself to go forward with this.

It is interesting because at the time I was working as a past life regressionist eight years prior and I can see how everything has its own divine timing. My children were little at that time and it would have not been the right time for me to get this information out as well.

S: Anything else about your current life as Jen that looks interesting?

J: I have to move. I have to move to Hawaii. It will be the change in energy that I need.

S: When should you move?

J: As soon as possible! I'm finally ready now! I've released this information, and I am finally free of all my ties to Atlantis.

S: How does doing a QHHT session affect this past version of yourself as Christie? Does this session affect her in any way?

J: It does! It brings peace to her, as well as peace to the other lifetimes in places where there is great anguish. This work that we are doing or any work like this strengthens your connection to your eternal self. It's like going to the gym and moving that muscle that you haven't used. And you finally get to a point where it is so defined that it is effortless to do this. And through this work you can hit this next level of understanding within yourself, around yourself, and about yourself and help with your ascension. But I have to tell you something very interesting.

S: What?

J: As I am looking in at my life, I see that everything is recorded and there will always be a record of everything, and it will be there for us at a later time. Everything is recorded in the akashic records, but more importantly, everything is recorded within the Sphinx and broadcast out. All of our lifetimes are stored within this communication, and I even see my life as Christie is broadcast out. Just like my planet with the spires, everything is so connected. It's available for other versions of ourselves on other planets to see so that they can keep tabs on our progress. **But for some reason I always see that there is a being named Three who will come back with information about the Sphinx.** I feel this is important, but I don't see anything else about this.

CHAPTER 18: THE SPHINX CONTAINS CONFIDENTIAL INFORMATION

Over the many years of being a QHHT practitioner I have seen and experienced a lot to where the sessions always keep me on my toes, but this one absolutely surprised me. Throughout writing this book it has been a journey for me as I searched for answers about the Sphinx. It was apparent that I had gotten too close to some confidential information in this session below. It is also important to note that Yana had never met Jen, nor knew about any of this information consciously, and yet, it is very similar to what Jen was saying in her sessions. Here is my shocking session with a woman named Yana.

S: What do you become aware of?

Y: I'm just standing right in front of the Sphinx, in front of its left bent knee. The sun is going down in the distance and there is a warm breeze that I can feel here.

S: And if you look down, can you see your feet?

Y: Yes. The sand is cool under my feet, and these are male feet. They're dark, and I look very Egyptian, or someone who is from this region. I have a white cloth wrapped around me. I look like I'm mid to late thirties or something.

S: And you are standing by the Sphinx? Is there anything that you notice that seems interesting about this?

Y: I'm standing very close to it. I'm almost staring right up to its face. And it's like it's communicating with me or something. I feel this very deep connection to it, almost as if it is connected to another realm, or something like that that I'm very familiar with.

S: Do you get a sense why you feel that way?

Y: I know that it has power, I sense and feel as if it communicates with me telepathically. If I put my ear right on the Sphinx, I can speak to it.

S: Tell me about that. Do you get a sense as to what you receive back from it?

Y: It reminds me of home. Oh, it's definitely connected to my home! I feel that the Sphinx is like a conduit between me and my home in another realm.

S: *Do you remember your home?*

Y: Vaguely. I know that it's in a different star system. And through the Sphinx, I feel that I have a strong connection to home. I want to remember my home!

S: *Ok, let's leave that scene and move back in time to when you were in the place that you call home. Just going back in time to when you were home and be there now. Tell me what you become aware of.*

I was not prepared for what happened next. As I asked to move Yana to see her (home) I was interrupted by what sounded like a different voice coming through her body. The voice had a different tone to it, almost methodical as it spoke. This is what it said.

Y: We have to interrupt this memory. We are the guardians of this information and Yana is not allowed to see her home planet at this time. We are showing her a spaceship with her people on it instead, but we can't show her the home planet at this time.

S: *Why?*

Y: It contains very confidential information. It's not for everyone to know. A lack of understanding is possible.

S: *What would happen if people had that information?*

Y: There would be a possibility for confusion. It is not yet time for humans to know.

S: *I see. What is this information that's confidential about?*

Y: Energy, and there is confidential information stored within the Sphinx connected to that particular planet.

S: *Oh, I see. Why would that be confidential?*

Y: It is not yet time for humans to know.

S: *Oh, why?*

Y: Because timing is of the essence, a lot of planning goes into when we will release certain things, and some of the energy and information connected to Yana's home planet are too confidential to share at this time.

S: *When will it be known?*

Y: Over the next couple of years. There will be events that arise that will show us that it is the appropriate time. We don't know yet when that time will be.

S: *Who am I talking to?*

Y: We are the guardians, the guardians of this information.

S: *What would happen if a person understood this confidential information?*

Y: They could become confused, but more importantly they could misuse this power.

S: *Oh. So, if people knew this information, they could misuse this power?*

Y: Certain people, yes.

S: *Oh, I see, because it has something to do with energy?*

Y: Yes. There are red crystals in connection to this and so we can't tell you more.

S: *Ok, I completely understand that, and I don't want you to tell me what it is that you are not allowed to tell, but I'm just curious if there is anything about the information that you could share?*

Y: We don't want this information to be intercepted and misused as we're waiting for the right time to release this information. We are the guardians of this information.

S: *I understand, and I don't want any information to get out that shouldn't, but why couldn't Yana see her home? She said she was hoping to see it. Would it affect her in some way if she saw it?*

Y: Because her home that you were about to take her to stores confidential information relating to the Sphinx, so we stepped in. However, we understand and greatly appreciate the work that you are doing, and we want to share with you the information that we are ready to release to humanity through you. We have been watching you and releasing bits of information to you that we do feel humanity can digest at this time. We would like to tell you more about the portal within the Sphinx.

Still a little confused by the experience I felt chills that I had been watched. (They) appreciated me! I understood that there were things that they couldn't share, but I was still excited to receive more.

S: *Ok, thank you very much. What would you like to tell me?*

Y: There's a portal within the Sphinx that allows one to time travel. It can only be used by people who know how to use it. Otherwise, it can be dangerous.

S: *How do you use it?*

Y: There are beings who use this portal to move in between different timelines. They play with time that way.

S: Oh. I had a client's higher self say that beings have come and changed time occasionally in a way where the majority of humans are unaware. Is that how they change time?

Y: Yes, they have done this occasionally. It is one of the ways that they secretly clean the Earth's oceans a little at a time without humans noticing.

S: Is this what causes the Mandela effect?

Y: It is part of it.

S: Tell me more.

Y: There are many probabilities for the Earth's trajectory. And the portal within the Sphinx is used to explore the different probabilities and future timelines.

S: What is the purpose of that? Why explore these?

Y: To understand the best path forward. At one point there was a probability that humans would destroy each other. That timeline, such as all timelines in this multidimensional reality has already played out. So there has been great effort to change this timeline, much effort to raise the vibration, much help, and now we are happy with our efforts and the probabilities we see in the Sphinx.

S: Are we moving on the best path forward?

Y: We're doing our very best to ensure that that's the case.

S: And this portal, it's used by beings to time travel. Is it used for any other reason?

Y: Some human researchers and scientists are already aware of this portal and are learning how to tap into this portal to understand it more.

S: How do they do that?

Y: Physics. There are a few human scientists on Earth who are aware and are beginning to experiment with this energy through the use of physics.

S: Is the energy beneficial to anyone, or no?

Y: Yes, very much beneficial. It would be beneficial for time travel - traveling through space and time; this portal can make it much more accessible. For example, you would not need vehicles to travel in between two points.

S: Like on other planets, or no?

Y: Oh, yes. Absolutely. And on the home planet.

S: Is there still a planet where that home planet was?

Y: Yes.

S: When Yana was first looking at the scene, she noticed that she was a man in Egypt; did he live on that home planet in a previous lifetime?

Y: Oh yes.

S: How was that life for him?

Y: We must be careful because there are files there about the red crystals. The red crystals were used in experimental capacity on Earth during the time of Atlantis and we can't let that happen again. It could be incredibly dangerous to Earth.

S: Why was it used experimentally on Earth?

Y: It was usurped, and we are the guardians of this information. So, we cannot let that happen again.

S: Okay. Thank you for protecting this information.

Y: We will bring back Yana and allow her to continue with her session with you now.

S: Ok! Thank you! Ok Yana let's go back to that scene where you are a man in the desert, standing by the Sphinx, be there now. What do you notice?

Y: There are people looking for me, but I fail to get a sense as to why.

S: Why are people looking for you?

Y: There are people in power that realize that I have something that they wish to have. I have important knowledge from the stars. This knowledge comes from my lineage, my connection to the home planet and to my people.

S: What type of knowledge do you have?

Y: I can communicate with my home planet. I also know fully who I am. I remember why I'm here. We are all from the stars, we are all one. We are all a part of one universal consciousness. But this information is sacred. I'm fully connected to a group called the guardians.

S: So, you have this knowledge, and it comes from your lineage. And people want this knowledge?

Y: They do. Mostly because they want to destroy anyone who has this knowledge. They do not want anyone to know this, because they want people to continue to be afraid and feel alone, in that way they can be easily controlled by this group of people.

S: *Tell me more.*

Y: One of the Pharoah's men that worked for the Pharaoh spotted my gift through clairvoyance, and he recognized my knowledge and connection with the Sphinx.

S: *Tell me more. Do they know this information?*

Y: Yes. They are very aware of some of it, but they don't know all of it. They know that the Sphinx is older than any of the pyramids, that it has been here since the beginning. But the Pharaoh's men don't know how it got here, or what type of people are linked with the Sphinx.

S: *Who are the people that are linked with the Sphinx?*

Y: I'm being told by a loud voice that that information is classified. That was really strange.

S: *Okay. All right. But there are people who are linked with this?*

Y: Yes. There are star people who are linked with the Sphinx.

S: *So, what happens after they find out you have this knowledge? What happens next to you?*

Y: They find me, tie me to a chair, and they torture me to death. They try to get the missing information that I have about the Sphinx, and I will not tell them.

S: *Why couldn't you tell them that information then?*

Y: It is and was absolutely classified because the information has been misused by this same group of people in the past.

S: *Tell me more.*

Y: This group has tried to use this information for pillaging, control, and murder. They perform a lot of dark rituals. They're in love with the darkness and the power most of all. They are a collective. They're from different planets; they unite through their common interests. If they knew more, it would give them more power. But I'm being told by a very loud voice right now that they don't have a footprint on this planet anymore! They are forbidden to come to Earth, so, their connection to Earth is through distance control.

S: *What happened? Why are they forbidden to come here?*

Y: They were here at one point, during these times in Egypt, but these dark beings were kicked out.

S: Tell me more about that. What happened?

Y: Agreements were made by different groups that were overseeing this human experiment. These groups form what some would call the Galactic Federation, and they became involved because these dark beings consistently broke agreements with Earth beings.

S: How? What were they doing?

Y: They were controlling humans through mind control. The Earth is a free will planet, and these beings broke that agreement and had to leave. However, they still have ways that they are controlling from a distance.

S: What are those ways?

Y: By manipulating people on the Earth to do their work for them, but their power is much more limited now.

S: Why?

Y: Because they are not able to be here. There's only so much they can do, and there's only so much time where they can do this. And I'm aware of this as a baby in this life; I am very aware that I am not from Earth.

S: Tell me about that.

Y: I am aware of my purpose at a very young age; I'm to be the eyes and ears of what is happening here on Earth, and I report this back to my home planet. I'm only going into this human life temporarily and I know that I have a job to do here.

S: Tell me about that.

Y: There are many groups who are currently working together to help the Earth become free of this tyranny.

S: Oh, I see, so they need people on the ground?

Y: They need those people on the Earth that subconsciously understand.

S: Is there anything else about this that you could tell me?

Y: There are many beings on the Earth now who are helping and who are planting energetic seeds here. We bring energy from the home planet here.

S: What happens when you bring the energy to Earth? Does this affect the Earth?

Y: Greatly. There's a reconfiguration of elements; it's hard to explain.

S: So, there are many beings here who are bringing energy to the Earth and that reconfigures something by them being here?

Y: Yes, it's changing the chemistry of Earth. When I grow up to be a teenager in that life in Egypt, I'm aware of this still, but I also become aware of my rage.

S: Why?

Y: I hate this planet!

S: Why?

Y: I don't like it here. It's so awful.

S: How do you spend your days there as a teenager? What do you remember?

Y: So much hard work. A lot of physical labor.

S: And you feel a lot of rage?

Y: Yes.

S: Are you still aware of your mission at this point? Or no?

Y: I am aware, but it makes me very angry. Why am I here? Why have they put me here in such an awful place?

S: Do you ever communicate this with them?

Y: It's getting harder and harder. because it's dense here on Earth. It's very dense. Very, very dense. It is easy to forget on this plane because it's so dense. That's what makes it awful. It's a planet of forgetting. I feel like it's a planet of ignorance.

S: Do you still communicate with your home planet? Do you tell them how you're so unhappy? Do they say anything to you?

Y: They asked me to remember why I'm here. Why I have chosen to come here.

S: Does that help you? Or no?

Y: It's difficult for me to remember why I chose to come here to Earth. And that is why I go to the Sphinx often because it reminds me of home and why I've come here.

S: *Why does the Sphinx remind you of home exactly?*

Y: The Sphinx is connected to my home. It is connected to several homes actually. It surpasses just one planet, it belongs to a collective, a lineage, and it cannot be corrupted. And I can feel it's consciousness, and this is the only thing that makes me feel better.

S: *How would you describe its consciousness?*

Y: It is pure, uncorruptible, and connected to a very strong energy field that it sits in.

S: Tell me more about this energy field.

Y: The energy field allows the Sphinx to be on Earth and also beyond Earth at the same time. There's an energy within it that connects it to the cosmos through the energy portal. This portal will be beneficial in the new Earth.

S: *And when you say the new Earth, do you mean the new Earth on this planet or the other Earth planet that is being seeded now?*

Y: While there is a different Earth that is being seeded now, I'm talking about the new Earth on this planet.

S: *Okay. Do you mean the information about entering the portal will be beneficial to humanity when Earth reaches its Ascension?*

Y: Yes.

S: *Okay. When do you see that happening?*

Y: When those dark energies leave their control over this place. I would like to find the others like me, the others like me on Earth that have come for the same purpose. They are here on the same mission. We have different parts to play, different jobs to do. I'd like to know where the others are! I see that they are there, but in different parts of the world. We're all in different parts.

S: *Do you get a sense as to why you are alone and everyone else like you is spread out throughout the world?*

Y: It is more efficient this way. It would not make sense for us to be in the same place, at the same time, but I feel very lonely. I understand why we cannot be together, but I'm upset because it makes me very lonely.

S: *I see that you wish you could have met somebody else like you. You know they're out there. It's very lonely for you.*

Y: Yes, all I have are these telepathic communications with the ship. And when you're on Earth, it gets very lonely.

S: Ok, let's move ahead in time to after you have left that lifetime and body behind. Now that you are out of that life what is the first thing that you notice?

Y: I'm on Earth again!

S: You're on Earth again. Tell me about that.

Y: I hate this place!

S: Do you know why you have come back?

Y: I'm beginning to forget more and more why I have come. My memories… they're going, they're starting to leave me.

S: Why?

Y: Because it's too dense to retain these memories and that is what happens here. I have to rely now on the ship to give me information, to help me remember, and to maintain that connection.

S: Do you still communicate with your ship?

Y: Yes, all the time.

S: Are you consciously aware of this?

Y: They mostly communicate with me during the nighttime when I sleep. That's when I can remember, but I'm not conscious.

S: At night when you're sleeping, you can remember?

Y: That's when they can communicate with me uninterrupted. That's when they give me healing and collect the information that I have for them, and they allow me to visit home and to be there for a time.

S: Do you remember visiting home?

Y: I remember glimpses. I remember the energy field on my planet.

S: How would you describe it?

Y: I know that it restores my field, my hope, my strength, and my resolve.

S: They take you to your home so that you can be restored, and you go back to this world?

Y: Yes, I don't remember this consciously, but it's very important for me to spend some hours there, visiting my home planet, every day.

S: So, you access it at night when you're sleeping?

Y: Yes, at night mostly, but anytime my conscious mind falls asleep.

S: Is there anything else about your planet that you notice through your glimpses of it?

Y: There is high frequency energy there that has many different purposes and uses, and I see many different colors of energy and frequency. I'm being told that I am not allowed to see anymore of this home planet at this time.

S: Because the information is confidential?

Y: Yes. It's not time. But there are many, many things that you can do on the home planet. There are many things you can do when you are not a human.

S: What kind of things can you do?

Y: When you are an energy form you can play and move all throughout the galaxy. You can perform many different tasks and bring different resources and energies and explore and distribute different things to different planets. I Enjoy different planets for the different things that they offer. There's a lot of movement that can happen. And I really miss this movement so much. This will be what the new Earth will be like.

S: Tell me about that.

Y: The voice just said that there will be this pure white energy, some may see it as blue or with a blueish tint, on the planet Earth. It is a very peaceful energy. Very healing energy.

S: Could I speak directly with this voice now?

Y: Yes, we are here.

S: What will this be like for humans?

Y: When the Earth evolves into this new Earth, people will see more beauty in everything because the color and the energy is of a higher frequency. So, beauty is intensified.
There's a lot of beauty on Earth. People are already tapping into this new Earth now.

S: How do people tap into the new Earth now?

Y: Through their awareness they can match the frequency of the new Earth, so it is quite possible for people to be able to be there now.

S: Why is there a lot of chaos happening on the planet now?

Y: There were mistakes that were made in the past, and all those involved, need to forgive themselves for these mistakes that were made in the beginning of seeding this planet this time around. There were very powerful energies that they did not know could be so destructive here, and there was a lot of suffering from the energy within the red crystals. The Earth beings were not ready to receive that energy and we have all learned from these mistakes and the destructions of Lemuria and Atlantis because of the misused power of the red crystals. So, we all need to let go of this. This was just an experience in this play of duality, where suffering exists, where darkness exists, where pain exists. Let go of those previous personalities and identities that you have experienced in other incarnations; they do not need to be held onto. Just like watching a movie, do you become the characters in the movie that you watch? Do you play those characters? No. You're simply watching a movie and identifying with a character for a certain amount of time. And once the movie is finished, the character is gone, it is not real. Once you begin to let go of these programs, these characters, these identities that you have made, your natural state will be returned. Your real self will emerge, and you will ascend.

S: What do people need to understand about the Sphinx?

Y: There are records within the Sphinx that will be of much greater importance to the human narrative in the not so far off future and we are already planning to release them to you then, but some of these records are highly confidential at this point in your history and that's the problem. Some of these records can be accessed, but not all of them will be accessed for this book we want you to release, and therefore we must release information to you in a way that is safe and not dangerous to the humans.

S: Are you the same grouping of beings who have been helping me gather this information?

Y: This is a collective effort, to share with you what is most important, and we will talk amongst ourselves, and will let you know what we can release to you in your next session. That is all for now.

CHAPTER 19: EARTH'S PROGRESS

After my session with Yana, we were both amazed and wanted to find out more about the information that should be put in this book. Yana agreed to do another session with me. Below is more confirming information to that which Jen recounted as well.

S: *What do you notice?*

Y: There is sand all around me, but I can see my feet. This might sound strange, but my feet don't look like human feet! And now I'm down here on Earth and there's nothing but sand under my feet.

S: *What about the rest of you?* How would you describe your body?

Y: (Laughing) I'm definitely not human. I suppose I look like an alien! My feet, well they have one really pointy toe. It's almost like I'm wearing a jumpsuit but it's very fitting to the body. I have two arms and two legs. And my head is also purplish in color. And my eyes are like, well alien's eyes. They're large. And my feet both have like this pointy shape to them.

S: *What does your jumpsuit look like?*

Y: It's all one color, purple, and it's so close to the skin that it looks like my skin but also functions as my clothes. There's a small design on the left breast pocket.

S: *What does this design mean to you?*

Y: It's just the symbol of the program I belong in. I measure, hold knowledge and report on what I see.

S: *What do you see around you if you look around yourself?*

Y: There's lots of sand, dunes, and I see a pyramid in the distance, but far off in the distance. It's interesting because I know that it's hot, but I don't feel the temperature because my suit regulates the temperature of my body.

S: *Are you carrying anything with you, or no?*

Y: Yes, I'm carrying some tools with me, but it's hard to explain, they're not physical tools. They're measurement tools. I'm equipped with technology that can measure and test. I'm going to use these tools when I get inside this pyramid.

S: *Did you acquire these measurement tools, or have you always had them?*

Y: I've been given these tools as I've been equipped specifically for this trip. This is the program that I'm equipped for.

S: *Can you tell me about that? What was that like getting equipped for this program? Do you remember?*

Y: Yes, I get a sense that there's a squadron, there's others like me on a ship not too far away actually. They're close but not at all what humans would define as close, the ship is not in this galaxy. The beings on the ship are watching me, however.

S: *How do they watch you?*

Y: They can see everything that I do. They're looking at me right now through a screen and they can see where I am in my surroundings. So, they can help to guide me. And in one sense they're using me almost as their eyes and ears, and also see what I'm doing.

S: *What do the beings on your ship look like?*

Y: They're like me. They look like they're all wearing the same suit; they all have purple suits.

S: *Do you get a sense of what your home is like or where you're from?*

Y: We come from a planet. I'm not sure where that planet is exactly, but the planet itself looks white.

S: *Is there anything on this planet that you notice? Or that you sense, or can remember?*

Y: It's definitely of a higher realm.

S: *What makes you say that?*

Y: Because of the white light, it's pure. It's pure white light and it's almost like as I get closer to the planet, the peace I feel is very, very deep.

S: *When you're on that planet, you feel very deep peace?*

Y: I get the sense that the beings here on my planet do what they wish and whatever they want. But all the beings are different than one another and some don't do anything. They enjoy just being in that pure energy and being in this space. There's a lot of beauty here on my home planet. It's like there are rainbows everywhere. There's a blue sky and there is grass and even rain, and everything is vibrating. All the colors, wow, they are vibrating too.

S: What kind of things do you enjoy doing there?

Y: I just sit a lot and enjoy the beauty and the feeling of oneness and the joy of pure beingness.

S: Do you think thoughts when you sit and just be, or no?

Y: I can if I want, but most of the time I don't have thoughts. It feels good to not have thoughts.

S: So, what made you come to Earth?

Y: I was recruited, there's a group of us. We volunteered to help the Earth in her ascension.

S: How did you get to the Earth?

Y: We have ships that can go to Earth easily and quickly.

S: What are your ships like?

Y: I see them very clearly but they're an interesting shape. They look almost like the shape of a pebble that has different creases on it. It's not a perfect shape at all, and there are little windows all around it.

S: And how does it fly?

Y: It does not need a secondary source to fly.

S: So, what happens now that you're on the Earth and you find yourself around all these sand dunes and the Pyramid?

Y: I'm walking through the pyramid now, and I know exactly where I'm supposed to go. I've been here before. There are computations that I'm going to have to make. This pyramid is very beautiful to me and it's the exact color of the sand. So, if I didn't know there was a pyramid here, it would look almost blended in with the surroundings, and from a distance, you wouldn't even see it. But when you get close, you see that there's a structure, and the texture of the pyramid is incredibly smooth.

S: What do you do inside the pyramid?

Y: Right now, I'm just touching the surface of it because this material is special. We don't have this material on our planet. I'm being told that the pyramid is built from the sand, the material of the sand. They created blocks out of the sand, and they put it together.

S: How?

Y: There are beings that can create density out of this sand material. Humans didn't build this pyramid. It wasn't our people either.

S: *And do you get a sense as to who did it, or no?*

Y: We know of them, but I don't get a sense that I'm that close to this group of people. I don't necessarily feel like I have a positive feeling toward them.

S: *Why is that?*

Y: I'm not so sure, but as soon as that feeling arises, it immediately neutralizes within my body. I can't remain in either negative or positive states, it just neutralizes. Emotions in this body are different than emotions in a human body.

S: *What happens next after you go inside the pyramid?*

Y: I walk through this entrance. And let's just say that the entrance is not an obvious entrance. It's not meant to be entered by just anyone because you have to shift yourself to become as light as energy to enter. Otherwise, I don't see a door. I'm inside the pyramid now, and there's…. it's so interesting. This pyramid is like a perfect mirror of itself. There is an underground pyramid that mirrors exactly the above ground pyramid.

S: *Tell me more.*

Y: My work will take place underneath this pyramid, in the pyramid under the ground.

S: *What is it like down there?*

Y: There's definitely something hidden here. And it's meant to be hidden. The upstairs part of the pyramid is just like a decoy, an empty room. It's the underneath side that contains - I'm trying to figure out what and I can't quite see. I'm trying to communicate with my ship now because I seem to be out of answers. Okay, I see, it contains information and there are tunnels on each side of the pyramid.

S: *What are the tunnels used for?*

Y: As an access doorway.

S: *How do you get into these doorways?*

Y: They're just behind the walls. There appears to be four tunnels going in each direction. There's a tunnel that also goes down directly into the Inner Earth. So, there are actually five tunnels. I'm being led into the tunnel that leads into the Earth…It almost seems to be like a labyrinth, a maze. And it's intricate, and it is all underground, and it goes very far underneath the Earth's surface.

S: What is the Labyrinth used for? Do you get a sense?

Y: It has several purposes, but one is for working on the soil. There are beings that work through these tunnels on the deeper layer of Earth.

S: Why do they work on the soil?

Y: Because if beings did not work on the soil, then there would be no more humans on this planet. There has to be a certain amount of minerals that is sustained within the soil, otherwise the soil is completely stripped. If we weren't maintaining this balance within the soil, then it would have turned into dust a long time ago.

S: What are these beings like that take care of the soil?

Y: They're all volunteers. They're from different planets.

S: Is this all over the Earth, or just underneath these pyramids?

Y: It's all over the Earth. But the pyramids are one particular access point. There are several pyramids that provide these kinds of access points. They are specifically positioned and there are six of them together all perfectly placed, and I just feel like there's so much science involved, and my brain can't explain it. But the arrangement is important, very important.

S: Without using science, why do you think that the placement is important?

Y: The pyramids are acting like portals. They're drawing energy from specific spots in the Universe. Not just this Universe, they are drawing energy from many specific sources. And the geographic placement with the angle is very important, so that it can properly be connected to these energy sources and draw energy from these sources. These sources are also bringing information back and connecting all of this information to the Sphinx.

S: What is the purpose of that?

Y: It's all about sharing the Earth's progress, providing updates to share how the work is unfolding. In a sense, it's like reading the temperature of the Earth.

S: What does the temperature of Earth look like now?

Y: Okay, I will ask. What I'm being told is that it looks good, we're exactly on time, it's going well. It looks like the Earth has been repaired, like it's had quite a bit of repair over time. It was near the brink of collapse at one point. Extra-terrestrials have changed time a little bit here and there so that they could clean up the oceans and the Earth. It's done in a way that many humans don't notice. Playing with time can be used, but the biggest impact is energy. The Earth has been bathed in a healing energy for quite some time.

S: What kind of energy do you mean?

Y: It's high frequency healing energy. It comes through every pyramid portal; the energy that's interacting through each of these is creating a prism of light. And that prism of light is interacting with these sources as well. And it's creating a complex geometric shape, and it even has compartments within it that are crystal like in nature. And the Earth is part of this healing space. The Earth has been included in this and that has helped the energy of the Earth to increase in frequency because of this.

S: Where does this energy come from?

Y: It's coming from everywhere even from the geometry within the Earth itself. I mean, obviously, these are high frequency sources. One of these sources is the central sun, so it's undoubtedly very powerful. But the reason that it works is because of the geometry, the placement of these portals connecting to one another to create a healing contraption, a very big one, one made to heal planets. The Earth is part of – I see a white, blueish film, all above and around the Earth. And the Earth is turning into a higher frequency planet. There is a connection between the Earth and my planet!

S: What is the connection between the Earth and your planet?

Y: It's that pure white, blueish light energy that my planet has. I see the same kind of white film starting to form around the Earth. I feel that our planet is part of this Earth's evolution. I'm seeing that your Earth is on its way to the same state of frequency that my planet has.

S: Is your planet the future of Earth? Or is it just a different planet?

Y: It's not the same. It's not Earth. It's one of the Earth planets. There are several Earth planets. And my planet has evolved to where it is now, as that high frequency energy has been there for a long time. And that will happen to this Earth.

S: So, this will happen to Earth, and Earth is evolving along the same trajectory?

Y: Yes, my planet and your Earth are connected along parallel lines and an energetic grid. My planet is connected to your Earth planet along this grid, along this timeline grid. If you can imagine a ladder with rungs, my planet is toward the top of the ladder, your Earth is somewhere right behind the middle, and there are a number of Earth planets all along each rung of this ladder and they're all evolving to higher and higher frequencies.

S: Is that just the way that they're supposed to go? Or the way that it works?

Y: It's a lineage of Earth planets that evolve along this trajectory, and this particular timeline is this Earth's pathway of evolution. And eventually, all evolve.

S: So, this Earth is evolving?

Y: Yes, there is still duality on this Earth, but it won't last much longer. Your planet is on its way out of duality.

S: *Was there a purpose to the duality?*

Y: Every Earth planet along this trajectory passes through a stage of duality in its infancy. That's just the way that it works.

S: *Tell me more about what is happening to this Earth.*

Y: There are versions of your planet along each step of the ladder so to speak, but once a planet reaches a certain frequency, it then jumps to the higher step of the ladder, a higher dimension. This is just the way that evolution works for these Earth planets. It's the way that my planet evolved. Now I'm going to try to get a temperature reading of Earth.

S: *Okay. How is this Earth's temperature?*

Y: There's a part of Earth that's still very sick. It's the equivalent of a human being with a very high fever. There's a sickness on Earth.

S: *What caused this sickness?*

Y: The consciousness of the dark beings that have been on this planet. They're extracting a lot. They're taking from the Earth like a parasite, sucking the Earth of its life. That's what has been causing the sickness. From a higher perspective it would look as if one side of the Earth is covered in this white, bluish light frequency, the other side of the Earth is still covered in this sickness.

S: *What parts of the Earth are covered in this darkness? Or does it depend on where there's a higher frequency or not?*

Y: Right now, there is a split, however, this white light frequency is slowly transcending into the other side consumed with darkness. And it's doing its best to work as quickly as it can, let's just say to heal the sickness. It looks like it may take some time because some parts are very sick.

S: *Will the whole planet be covered in the white light eventually?*

Y: Yes, it doesn't have a choice. But if I were to look at the sickness, which I'm going to do for a moment now…. I'm seeing that there's lots of elements happening here.

S: *What's happening?*

Y: There are different species of beings that are asserting their control on this Earth from warring planets. So, they're of that negative frequency. And they are still affecting Earth. They are trying to hold their ground.

S: Why?

Y: Because they enjoy raping the Earth of its resources.

S: Why?

Y: Because that's what they do. They go from planet to planet and do this. They've had control on the Earth for a long time. So, they've been taking from Earth for a long time. And they feel that it's their right to do this, that this is what they do.

S: Is it their right to take?

Y: We don't judge what is right or wrong. They're operating from that perspective. That's what they know, what they can see. So, from their perspective, they are correct, and it is their right.

S: When they come to take, do they affect humans as well?

Y: In a lot of ways. One of the main reasons that humans are sick is because of trauma inflicted by these wars. And the energy that they're bringing here is very dense and dark. So, it's just even through their energy frequency that they're polluting a massive part of the environment here. They pollute through their frequency; it's very dense. Their mentality is very dark as well.

S: And why did they come to this Earth?

Y: There were a lot of resources to be had on this planet when the fear virus arrived, and the Earth didn't really have any defenses.

S: What's their favorite resource?

Y: Humans are a resource for them. They use humans through their fear. And so, there is enslavement, there is enslavement happening through fear.

S: Can you tell me about that? How does that work?

Y: This has been going on for a very long time. Humans were used as slaves during ancient Egypt. It was a very common thing. And this kind of lineage of slavery has become, you know, just very systemic here. Humans are not really being used for physical labor anymore. These warring beings have already built what they needed to build.

S: How are humans used now?

Y: Through mind control. That is the predominant tool that is being used. The human mind is very, very easy to manipulate and has very few defenses, and so it is easy to control.

S: Tell me more. What is happening with these warring beings?

Y: These dark beings are now trying as hard as they can to control as many as possible because they themselves are reacting out of fear, because they can see this white light frequency is taking over this Earth planet. They know it, they see it, and they're trying to control how long they can keep this darkness here. So, the more people are plugged into this darkness the longer it will take for light to be absorbed. These warring dark beings are just buying time, and they're going to try to drag it out as long as possible. It's what they do. They want their influence to remain on Earth as long as they can. But they all know that once the frequency gets to a certain point, they will not be able to stay here anymore. Their energy will no longer be compatible.

S: They won't be able to stay? So why not allow the white light frequency to absorb them as well so that these dark beings can evolve too?

Y: A few of them have chosen that, a number of these entities are choosing that now. But of course, not all of them are ready to evolve. They're not ready to stop playing their game, they're having too much fun. And they want to continue to do that. And they will do that on another planet when it's time for them to leave. They will find another planet that is easy to infiltrate just like Earth, a planet that is open.

S: I have a question. What about people that refuse to wake up and accept this light energy?

Y: There are humans who are not ready to evolve, and they will be placed on planets where they're more compatible with that frequency. There will always be a compatible host or place to match the frequency of those that don't wish to evolve. And that is in progress, that is part of this whole transition, placements are being found for those beings that are not ready to evolve.

S: Okay, but Earth is definitely making her transition?

Y: Yes. Earth is definitely making this transition. It's in progress, and the Earth will not split into two planets, it will remain as one planet of a higher frequency.

S: Can you tell me more about this dark side? What are they doing now on our Earth?

Y: There are multiple tools for mind control that are being employed now. The media is one, the virus and vaccine are another.

S: How is the virus one exactly? Is there really a virus or was that just something that was made by these dark players?

Y: There is definitely a biological component to this virus. But I'm being shown that the biological component is relatively small compared to the psychological component. If enough people believe that something is dangerous, then it will become dangerous. And I'm being shown the same is true with the vaccine. These are props, they are psychological tools for warfare.

S: Vaccines only, or also the virus?

⭐ Y: The virus and the vaccine - they go hand in hand, they were always meant to be introduced together as a bundle. Because the mind is so powerful, especially now that the frequency of the Earth is rising, the mind has an even greater impact - what we think and what we believe, is manifested more quickly. The more people believe in the destructive and harmful effects of these tools, the more it will make them destructive and harmful. So, it's working very well for these dark entities the way that it's playing out, because there's such a strong belief in it in - in this poison. I'm being shown that it takes stronger minds to not fall into this theatrical scenario that is being fed to the masses - the fear of the vaccine itself is also part of their agenda, because it's just as destructive. The fear itself is destructive, if not MORE destructive than the biological component.

S: *What about the people that received the vaccine and then had side effects? What about those people?*

Y: For those that wanted it, and have chosen it, and have no fear involved, then there may or may not be biological impact on the body. But it's much, much, much more beneficial
to have a positive intention whilst taking the vaccine. It's the fear that they're playing on more than any biological component at this point. Although if someone believes strongly that the vaccine has detrimental effects, if that is part of their belief system, whether they're conscious of it or not, then I'm being shown that it will be more likely to have those effects because that's how strong our mind is.

S: *Is manifestation so high because of this white, blueish light?*

Y: That is exactly correct. We have much more power now, in terms of our mental abilities to manifest because that frequency is already here. The mental component is very powerful right now because this Earth has now been classified as one of those 'manifesting' planets. You can manifest here more quickly because of the frequency. That can be used either for good or for bad. It is really important now to understand just how powerful your beliefs and your thoughts are.

S: *What sort of advice would you give a human to help them learn to master their thoughts and emotions?*

Y: Well, right now, this is the single most powerful thing that that the human can do is to understand the power of thought, the power of belief. And it really is belief and thought that constitute consciousness and dictates how consciousness manifests on the physical plane. There are so many different ways to do it depending on the human being's preference. Meditation is crucial now. The ability to recognize your true identity is crucial. You are not just the mind body unit; human beings have to understand and move beyond their identity. It helps to have higher awareness.

S: *So, you said meditation is crucial as well as understanding who you truly are? What if people don't meditate? Is there another way that a person can control their mind during this manifestation period?*

Y: The thoughts that people think on a daily basis are very important because they will create the reality that they will be living in. This is like a two- or three-year period that we're talking about. So, whatever it takes, is what you should use. Don't allow negative thoughts to stay in your mental space.

Instead, fill your mental space with thoughts that you enjoy and that you like because your thoughts and your beliefs will show up in your physical environment in a very big way. The individual should do whatever it takes to release negative thoughts without causing physical impact to the body. If a being is doing a lot of drugs to release the thoughts, then that's going to also have a negative impact because the body can't handle toxic material. But find, choose, any way that works for you. One easy way for people who don't have a strong meditation practice is simply to be in nature. If you can walk barefoot on the ground on your Earth, you can connect to her. That is another way that you can be fed high frequency energy. When you are being fed high frequency energy through the Earth, then you are much better off, in terms of the kind of thoughts that enter your mind. You can also give the Earth your negative thoughts, she is taking them, she is playing her part to help, so you can give whatever energy away to the Earth that you don't want, and she will absorb it. You can even visualize your thoughts leaving from the top of your crown chakra just seeping out and then being absorbed by the Earth or seeping out through the bottoms of your feet, and you can just visualize them leaving, exiting your system.

S: Thank you. Could you tell me more about this light? I've heard that it's also helping to release fear by shaking things up within the human, to reveal the negativity, and the fear, so that it can be released. Is this correct?

Y: That is correct. There is so much help on the planet for the humans at this time. There is also the help from the inner Earth, the inner layers within. There are not many dark beings on the inside layers of the Earth, and so the white light frequency can travel through many of these layers with ease, and it is doing all it can to travel in all different ways to get to a being that is receptive. Anyone that is receptive to it, it will penetrate. But at the same time, there are distractors. The media is very strong, there are beings that are very tightly connected to their fear. And for these beings that are so unaware of the truths within themselves and the higher realms, I see them being consumed by this darkness more and more.

S: So, it's easier for them now to be consumed by this darkness?

Y: Yes, but they don't have that much longer to be consumed. I mean, I get the sense that you need to act quickly, however, you need to know that anyone can wake up at any moment because that is the right of any being in existence. So, for a being that has extremely strong desire to awaken, they can choose to do so at any time. There are those – perhaps we can call them "on the fence;" and who are still unaware of their own divine power, then they're easy prey. And for that reason, they will likely not escape from this mental trap, because it's too easy. There are too many things that are being used to keep someone in a state of fear. There are many different tools being used. And if the human is not able to see through them then they don't really have much of a chance. The more people there are that are aware of the higher realms, aware of the higher consciousness, and the more that they connect, the more understanding there is, the more opportunities there will be for others to awaken.

S: Oh, so we're helping to create the environments for others to awaken?

Y: Yes. Each person helps by awakening themselves. Each person helps by what they think about throughout their day. If, let's say, a large group of five thousand or more, are creating the scenarios in their mind that there will be a massive opportunity for others to awaken then you are influencing that reality to take place, because many of you are believing in it.

S: Oh, so manifestation can happen in many different ways now on this planet?

Y: Yes, it does. And it goes down to what people believe, think, and feel.

S: Thank you so much. Do you have any other messages for humans?

Y: Compassion during this time is important. There are souls at so many different stages of evolution and awareness. There are many beings that are very deeply asleep while there are souls who are on the brink of full enlightenment on this planet right now. There's just so much diversity that someone who is on the brink of awakening can be living next to someone who is lifetimes away from awakening. You have many beings living in completely different paradigms. And the natural tendency is to judge where others are in their evolution when it's not the same place that you are in. And both sides are doing this. And so, the less judgment there is, the better this transition will go. It's not that judgment is going to do anything terrible but releasing judgement will make things easier for you all as individuals. So just unburden yourself by allowing yourself not to be so judgmental. You will help support your own awakening that way. Hold the compassion. Feel that compassion. Because what is happening here, is very unusual in many ways. **And one day you will understand just how lucky you are not to be asleep at this time**. Because those who are 'asleep' are caught in a very difficult situation. They simply did not have enough time to learn the lessons at the pace that human beings learn. At this point if you are not already awake then you have to be a really fast learner, however, the environment on Earth is ripe for learning quickly. There is a lot of help, a lot of very, very benevolent powerful energy that exists on this planet right now. But you have to be open enough to even want to use it and to believe that it's there. Some have not gotten to that place of openness, and so they are stuck in their fear, unable to tap into those higher realms. But even they will see very quickly, once they pass into spirit form, they will see exactly what's happening on this planet. And they will understand this boundary between dark and light right now. They may not understand or believe that there is a battle of dark and light happening while they are in the human form. For some it will take death to see it. But once they die, they will see it right away. All souls passing out of body now, out of this lifetime, are waking up quickly after death.

S: Some people are waking up after they die?

Y: Yes, they can have the opportunity at that stage. So, don't worry about those who are dying because they too have a choice.

S: Tell me more about that.

Y: They have a choice and if they do not feel ready to wake up upon death, they will be relocated. However, that will depend on their level of consciousness, their level of awareness upon death. But I will say this, that those who are dying are seeing with very clear eyes exactly what is taking place right now on this planet. So, in one sense, it's easier to 'awaken' after death than it was in the past.

S: It was harder to wake up after death before this?

Y: Well, let's just say that the environment is ripe for deeper clarity now. So, for this Earth, there is a plane that exists, the life in between lives, and that plane is also infused with higher frequency energy, just like on this plane.

S: You said before that you would let me know what information you can release for this book, especially about the Sphinx.

Y: We have released to you that the Sphinx acts like a radio signal between Earth and its planet of origin as well as multiple other planets. It is constantly receiving new messages from multiple planets at this time.

S: How does it receive this signal?

Y: The Sphinx has its own consciousness. It is a conscious being. Just as other conscious beings, it has chosen to carry out its mission here on Earth.

S: What is the Sphinx's mission?

Y: The Sphinx is here to act as a transporter, radio signal and a portal to receiving many different languages and frequencies. Therefore, many beings from many different planets use the Sphinx.

S: Can you tell me more about that?

Y: In a sense the Sphinx was placed here as a base, even before any living beings arrived. We needed a radio signal set up here as a connector. The Sphinx connects us to many different bases and planets that are involved in the work here on Earth. The Sphinx was set up for that purpose. The Sphinx has remained at a very high state of consciousness. For the entire duration of its time on Earth, it has remained unimpeded. Humans can communicate with the Sphinx.

S: How?

Y: They can practice communicating with the Sphinx telepathically within their mind. You can practice tuning in to that specific signal. It is there for everyone who would like to learn, but by doing this, it is possible to have more communications with the rest of your family who does not live on this planet. This will make your job on Earth easier.

S: What does the Sphinx contain within it?

Y: It contains items that are highly valued for Earth beings. The contents are more linked to Earth's work; it is less important to us and our work.

S: Anything else you would like to tell us about the inside of the Sphinx?

Y: The Sphinx is a doorway to the underground. You can even imagine a stairway underneath the

Sphinx that goes to an underground world.

S: What is this underground world exactly?

Y: There are some colonies of hybrids and other beings there.

S: And are they underneath the Sphinx?

Y: No, not directly underneath the Sphinx. They are located closer to the core of the Earth. There is an incredible amount of heat there, so their bodies have evolved very differently. Life within the core of the Earth has a much different environment, almost as though they are on a different planet altogether. The consciousness is also of a much higher quality.

S: Anything else about the Sphinx that you would like to speak about?

Y: The Sphinx contains portals to many different dimensions. You could even say that to enter into the Sphinx is to pass through these dimensions. Hence, it is not what we would call a safe place for humans to go to, unless you know how to work with that energy.

S: How does one work that energy?

Y: In one sense, one must enter the Sphinx in their energetic form, not their physical form, so that there will not be as much of a risk involved.

S: What will happen if you enter physically?

Y: You may end up physically leaving this dimension and entering another, without knowing where you will be going. This is the same phenomenon that has happened in the Bermuda triangle.

S: So, you recommend entering the Sphinx in a nonphysical form?

Y: Yes, you can tune in to this signal.

S: Can you tune into this signal within the Sphinx right now?

Y: We always have communication with the Sphinx.

S: If you look at the records within the Sphinx is there anything about Mars in there?

Y: Yes, the records are contained there within the Sphinx about Mars, what do you want to know?

S: What happened to the people on Mars? Why was Mars destroyed? Why is it not habitable anymore?

Y: There are various reasons. There was warring amongst its people.

S: How was it destroyed?

Y: Eventually there was a complete depletion of natural resources on the planet. Some of the people were evacuated as the destruction occurred and some were not. It looks like there was a collision of some sorts in space and that created devastating results.

S: Are there people on the planet now who have trauma from that lifetime or no?

Y: Yes, there are many people on the Earth now that remember that lifetime or that were living then. It looks like there was a collision near Mars and this collision had catastrophic results that left the planet uninhabitable. Some were rescued and left to go back to their home planet, but many died in the aftermath of the destruction. The warring factions on that planet also created chaos to the point where many decided to go separate ways.

S: What is the history of your planet? Was it like Earth?

Y: At this time, it is very different than Earth. There is little that our two planets have in common.

S: What about the history? Was it different than Earth?

Y: At one point it was similar to Earth. Initially there were various forms of us in the beginning and many experiments, and there were also similar seeding methods and figuring out the right genetics.

S: What genetic form worked the best for your planet?

Y: A form like a Sasquatch. There are many similarities to the ones on your planet. The Sasquatches on Earth are more local to Earth than humans are.

S: What do you mean?

Y: A human's genetics are more mixed.

S: Why don't humans and Sasquatches interact?

Y: They are different species and the Sasquatches and humans on Earth both live in different paradigms.

S: Are there any other similarities between your planet and Earth?

Y: We are similar to Earth in that there were different variations of genetics that survived through different gene pools. There were several types of beings living there at one time.

S: Did your planet have the fear virus like the Earth does?

Y: Yes, it is common. Not all planets have that virus, but within our history it did happen on our planet as well as a necessary part of our evolution, but we evolved past it.

S: How did you evolve?

Y: There are energies on our planet that can sustain multiple paradigms at once. We evolved to a higher paradigm. There were many different portals on my planet where there were energies that represented different dimensions on a planet where there was no conflict.

S: Could you tell me more about how the Sphinx communicates with your planet?

Y: There is communication, but a lot of that information is confidential and can't be shared at this time.

S: Ok, I understand, but could you tell me why that is confidential?

Y: It has been agreed to not share what is being shared from my planet to your Sphinx.

S: Ok. Only tell me what you are allowed.

Y: Soon humans will understand that there is something coming from my planet that will be important for Earth. It's part of the preparation for what is to come.

S: What can you tell me about what is to come?

Y: Earth's frequency is rising and at a certain point there will be a lot more diversity here. Many different beings of aliens will inhabit Earth alongside humans.

S: When?

Y: Not too long from now.

S: What will the other beings do when they inhabit the Earth?

Y: They will help to rebuild sustainable communities. They will introduce their technology. They will help humans.

S: Why hasn't this happened before?

Y: It was not time. There needed to be higher awareness amongst the humans before this could happen.

S: So, something from your planet is important for Earth?

Y: Yes, it is an energetic and a highly classified type of free energy, which we cannot describe at this time. However, timing is of importance because there are people on the planet now that don't want this alternative source of energy. They would try to repress it. This form of energy can be highly volatile and could be easily misused as it was during the times of Atlantis. It's a matter of raising the consciousness on Earth so that energies like this would never be misused.

S: What is Yana's mission exactly?

Y: We cannot reveal everything so we are determining what can be revealed at this time. Part of her mission is to help support the healing of humans as they transition to this new Earth. It can be hard for some who choose to remain here. Mostly because they are holding on to memories and holding onto what things used to be, so there will be a need to help and support the expansion of the belief system of humans.

S: What is her role in the new Earth?

Y: She has a role in developing Earth space technologies. The technologies in terms of farming and other energy source technologies from her home planet are within her genetic code. There are many beings on the planet with their own contribution to the new Earth that lay dormant at this time, but Yana will help to begin to develop and identify these. She will also work with others; younger souls being born on Earth now who are connected to the Earths' intelligence. She will work with some of them.

S: What will she do with them?

Y: She will provide a safe school for these children, and she will help them to harness their gifts which are related to earth-based technologies. The free source energy will be a part of it and there will be other people developing that as well. She will assist with the initial research and development to establish these technologies and the science behind them. She carries this wisdom from other planets stored within her DNA.

S: It seems like there are many other people with this information as well.

Y: There are many who are here to support the stabilization of the frequency of Earth. Many of them are really here more for the Earth. They anchor in the frequencies and are helping to stabilize frequencies through their chemistry, their body. Many of them are like vessels for higher awareness. Many of them work with inner Earth kingdoms because the inner Earth is a big part of this process.

S: Why?

Y: The inner Earth kingdoms are ancient and have been here for so long. They are working alongside many different alien volunteers to stabilize the frequencies on this planet. It had to be done from the inside out of the core to the outer layers, so that it would be stable.

S: After the extra-terrestrial beings start coming to Earth and live amongst these humans, will these volunteers still come into a human body, or no?

Y: No, they will not need to take on a human body anymore to live on the planet Earth. There will be more diversity on the Earth's surface because aliens will not need to take on the human suit as often.

S: Some of these volunteers describe themselves as miserable being in a human body on the Earth at this time. Do you have any advice for them?

Y: Focus on the outcome of all of this. Remember the goals that we have here and understand that your work will not be for nothing. And they can access their home planets by telepathically communicating with the Sphinx.

S: What are the goals we have here?

Y: The goals are to allow and support this planet to ascend and support any humans who wish to ascend with it.

S: How do these people communicate with the Sphinx exactly? Could you tell me more about that?

Y: I feel there is a being named Three that has come before and is back again who has this information about the Sphinx. This being knows the secrets within the Sphinx and will share them with humanity again.

As Yana said this, I could hardly believe what I was hearing! This Three had been brought up multiple times! Who was this being?

CHAPTER 20: THE FAIRY REALM

I'm always amazed at the information that comes through these sessions and how similar this information is throughout the higher selves of multiple clients. Here is another example and another session with a woman named Mary who remembered a lifetime as a fairy.

S: What do you become aware of?

M: There are little flags on garlands that are linked from one tree to another all over the place. There is a forest full of them, and it looks like a beautiful, little quaint village.

S: What else do you notice?

M: I feel like I'm somewhere where everything is so very comfortably familiar. It feels calming and safe and like home. And it feels like I'm in a miniature doll house, it's so intricate and beautiful. I know there are others here because I can hear what sounds like laughter, but I don't see them. It's like they are all doing something. We are fairies!

S: You said that it feels like home?

M: I belong here. It feels magical, magical is the best way to describe this place.

S: Do you have a body here?

M: I have little feet. They look like human feet, but they are really tiny and small, and I have something that looks like a leather slipper on them. The slippers feel like skin, like they are made just for me and fit perfectly. My skin has a slight greenish, shiny tint to it. I can see my legs, they are shiny, and so are my arms.

S: Are you holding anything in your hands, or no?

M: I have a little mirror, it's like a little handheld mirror that hangs off of my waist.

S: Is there a purpose for this mirror?

M: It's for directing light, and for moving in and out of layers and dimensions, to travel. They are showing me that there is light that is coming through the trees. I can hold up my mirror and see the light bouncing off of it, and I can see others that look like me who are holding up their mirrors too. So, it looks like we collectively do this, to bounce the light back and forth, into the center. There's a crack in the center that looks almost like a fabric being ripped, but it's an actual opening that you can walk though.

S: What is it like to walk through this?

M: It's like walking through a door. It's bright. I know that this is how we move to other locations. Sometimes we have to go to other places to do work, to gather, to visit. We don't have vehicles, so this is how we travel.

S: Why do you have to travel?

M: So that we can be in other realms. We deliver crystals to other places. They look reddish, like a red crystal. And we carry them in baskets.

S: Where do these red crystals come from?

M: For some reason there's someone who's speaking to me. I don't see them but as you were talking there's a voice saying to me that they're very powerful and special red crystals and we harvest them and shine them. Because of where these crystals are from, they're healing. We drop them in places and leave them in areas, I want to say dimensions, but I'm being told that worlds are a better way to describe it. We drop these in other worlds. I'm also being told that the mirrors are what we really use. For generations humans think we use wands because they see sparks of light when they see us, but they are mirrors! They're reflective, they aren't wands at all.

S: Does this voice that is talking to you have anything else to say?

M: I know who this is; it's a part of me. It's my guide, my inner guidance. I hear it very clearly and it tells me things that I need to understand. My life feels very simple and free here.

S: How do you spend your days there?

M: By doing regular human things, but I'm also very light and very healthy. There are no worries about disease. I last a very long time here.

S: Tell me more. Why is that?

M: Because I'm very aware that a body is necessary to do certain things, but I know that my body is only here for a certain period of time, and when my experience is over, I go back into the spark. It's like being part of the mirror again, and it's no different because I feel exactly the same. When I leave my body after living a life, I still think the same. It just feels like I just keep going on and on and we're all ok with that.

S: Do you change forms, or do you go on as the same being?

M: The voice that is in my head, the voice that is behind me, tells me what I am going to do next, where I need to be next.

S: *When you go about getting the crystals, do you get a sense as to where they come from?*

M: Sometimes they are in places where there was water. These places are not being described as Earth, but other versions of Earth. There are other beings in the Universe that treat some of these crystals like gold. They have been hidden from humans.

S: *Why were they hidden?*

M: Because in the wrong hands they are dangerous, and some beings are not capable of doing the healing work or having compassion for others. But these red crystals also contain knowledge, and it is knowledge that we would prefer not to get into the wrong hands.

S: *You harvest them, use your mirrors, and sprinkle them? Can you tell me more about that?*

M: Sometimes we leave them near other beings who need them. When we change form, when we leave our lives, we recognize all other beings as family and as beings that have a job to do. So, sometimes we use these crystals to help those who need help, or we help the environment, and sometimes we even use the red crystals to help with travel.

S: *How do these crystals assist with travel?*

M: Physical beings who are able to leave their conscious bodies, travel for many purposes and these crystals are encoded with numbers and information to help them reach certain destinations and locations.

S: *Where are these crystals from originally? You said that some of them are harvested?*

M: They are from many different planets.

S: *What do these crystals do on other planets?*

M: They have universal knowledge, and they record history. I notice that I'm very happy here. Everything is so fun and colorful, and there is laughter in the air.

S: *What do you do for fun?*

M: We race, we fly, it's so much fun. We're all family here.

S: *Tell me more about your family. Do you have a mother and father there?*

M: It's not like that. We choose who we want to live with, we don't have specific people that we identify as mother and father. But we are aware of who cares for us when we are in younger stages. I'm not sure how we are born. It feels like there is a physical experience, but it doesn't feel the same as a human experience.

S: Do you remember what it was like to be born?

M: I'm being shown an egg that has a holographic look to it. These eggs are all over the place here, there is a field full of them.

S: Where do the eggs originate?

M: They just appear by taking form; they look like they are created.

S: Do you feel as if someone creates you or do you feel that you create yourself?

M: It feels like I create myself with assistance and it feels very independent. But the voice that is with me is telling me that I will be ok as I'm experiencing myself being born.

S: Why does that voice tell you that it will be ok?

M: Because coming into that holographic reality is new. It's another new experience because I've come from somewhere else again. But my memory is intact! I don't forget my past lives like I do when I'm a human. I don't feel like I'm being cut off from more information. This is a new experience for me, but as I grow and get stronger in this hologram, I start to get more curious and settled. I know I'm going to be here in this life as a fairy for a while. But I still have memories of being other places and being other beings.

S: Tell me more about the memories that you still have as you come into this new life as a fairy?

M: I remember what it was like to be a cell. I remember being transferred from my old self as a different being that is very extra-terrestrial in nature. I can see this being laying on a table and it looks like something is being extracted from the arm.

S: The being on the table is you. What happens next?

M: Looks like a cell in an octagon shape is taken out of this extra-terrestrial being that I once was and put inside these little egg-like capsules and there is an ultraviolet type of light. Part of me as a cell is being placed into one of those eggs, while part of me as this extra-terrestrial being still exists.

S: What is that experience like?

M: It's an interesting experience to see my DNA transform into this fairy self. This is me going into what I'm being told is the past.

S: You're going into the past?

M: I'm going into a place that already existed and there are many of us who go there. We come from all over the place. We show up in these little eggs.

S: You said that you are going into a place that already existed?

M: Yes, because we are changing the timelines. That's why we go into the past.

S: Why does this change need to take place?

M: To save the humans on Earth.

S: Why do you need to save the humans on Earth?

M: They can't save themselves. So, we change something within the timelines to save them. We are bringing forth information. Information travels in many forms and this information helps by bringing forth other options. The information helps to create splits in the timelines. And they are showing me, I can see, what looks like a graph with what looks like light moving all across these lines showing the importance of moving this information that is full of light. Moving light does not interfere with the rules, and we can use this light information technology to give humanity a better chance.

S: What are the rules that you need to follow?

M: Not interfering with experience is important. There are plans for humanity. It's not just about Earth, there are many plans that have taken place on other planets. Earth is just the focus that this part of me is aware of.

S: Why do you need a rule that says to not take away from experience?

M: Because the process of change must come authentically and not synthetically. I'm being shown that interference happened before on Earth. There have been universal wars. Other beings and other forms of consciousness fought for control on other planets, and they wanted to have control of Earth as well, not Earth exactly, but humanity. Earth will always be fine. Humanity has options now. There was a timeline where humanity didn't have options, and now there are options. And now there will be less casualty in the timeline that is present. This is one of the timelines we changed. A lot of the work that has been done was work that had to be rectified because there were beings that have made mistakes. If something happens to Earth, it affects many other parts of the Universe like a domino effect.

S: What does the present timeline look like?

M: **The present timeline includes the agreement of many souls to leave the Earth right now as causalities so they can return to their stations, to their spots. And when they return, they can return in their true form, without the need of a human body.** Some of these light beings will lead the way for Earth and consciousness to ascended.

S: *So, there's an agreement for these casualties to take place because casualties are needed so that these beings can return to their real bodies and positions, in order to be leaders as Earth ascends. And you said that that the current timeline looks better?*

M: There is less destruction, but there is still what looks to be two to three years of change. There may be some food shortages, but there won't really be shortages. It just looks like an argument over transportation and money. This may or may not happen because timelines change.

S: *Is there anything to do to prepare for this in case?*

M: Keep a supply of nonperishable foods and have different resources of finances at hand. There may be some necessity for cash at this time. It doesn't look like this will last for a long time.

S: *If this does happen, what is the purpose?*

M: Strings are tightening around those that work with an archaic type of system on Earth that are fed by power and greed.

S: *Why?*

M: Because there is change that is occurring on the Earth that has already started to take place, and there will be a transference of power. We will say that a balance is occurring in the consciousness that allows a more feminine energy to take a leadership role. Therefore, the masculine energy that is about greed and power can no longer have control or ethically be able to stay. As the strings are tightened, things will start to feel a little bit harder because the push back is a little bit harder. But that is necessary because the more that energy is pushed in the corner the harder it will bite back before it gives up.

S: *So, do we have to worry that these warring beings will take over the planet?*

M: No. The light has already been successful, but the current timelines you are in are playing out the physical steps that it needs to go through.

S: *Wait. So, have we already done this?*

M: Yes, there are parts that are being repeated in some time loops. However, this is a new stream of energy.

S: *Have we done this on other planets before?*

M: Yes, many times.

S: *So, you said it would be about two years till the chaos is over?*

M: Yes, but again that is just a possibility and in the future potentials there may be some natural disasters. They would be a result of the Earth changing its frequency, and as it does so there are shifts.

And so, this is part of the cleansing of some of the old energy. We don't see catastrophes, but we see damage and some loss of life. There are many who take advantage of certain situations that are occurring on Earth. Some systems, banking, pharmaceutical, education, and other large systems are in a time of fluctuation and change. These big companies like to take advantage of fear and fear of change. And so yes there is change and yes there may be shortages, they are all working together for the purpose of making money for these big companies. So, this will be something that society, especially in the western culture, will see that they have to work through deciding what is most important and what they can live without. This will also help society clear out the need for too much.

S: What about people's mortgages and houses? Will there be an agenda to repossess them if these people can't pay?

M: No, we see that there will be some change, and there is help that is going to come in, because we do see that there is eventually a balance of homeownership, and even a lowering of cost for homeowners.

S: Do you mean within the real estate market?

M: In the future potentials it looks like the banking structure of home ownership will make a change. This is not going to be a change that will occur in the next two years although we will see some signs of this change. We can say that the cost of homes will start to decrease and level themselves out. But there will be assistance that will come forward and help those with exorbitant loans.

S: Where does it look like this assistance comes from?

M: From new leadership.

S: When do you see this happening?

M: It has already started taking place. We have the shift of not only new souls coming in, but we have the shift of walk-ins taking place now. A walk-in is a soul that takes the place of a living soul without the living soul having to leave their earthly bodies and pass over. There are many walk-ins coming into a physical body that has already grown and gone through life experience. So, the walk ins are coming into a physical form that is already ready to be able to take on a challenge in a mature form. Some of these walk-ins will be the new leaders. These will be leaders that are seeking more of a group mentality. This will be something that we will see more of over the next five years.

S: So, it looks promising, correct? What about the souls that come back in their true form to be leaders?

M: That will happen as well and yes, although what we like to remind people is that there are things that are difficult to understand for the human mind. And as the human mind sees things it wants security to know that it will not have to go through any of these hardships or losses. These are only perceived losses, and they are to get to a better position. We say that sometimes these things are necessary to go through as there is still a physical experience that is taking place. And not all things will jump from one stage to another without the experience of loss. **So, although there will be some things that will take place that will give humans the idea that it is not going in the right**

direction, our advice is to say to hold on, hang in there and stand with hope. Because a new world is being born. And for a new world to be born there will be labor pains.

S: Well wouldn't it be beneficial to warn people?

M: We're not here to create fear. So, although it is a smart idea to always be prepared, we would say that being prepared and not paranoid is extremely important. Balance.

S: But there is still a possibility that there won't be any shortages or disasters, correct?

M: That is correct. There are so many timelines that can still occur. There is a quickening to the energy so even as we speak this right now there could be changes that take place that do not give formulation to a food shortage.

S: What about the vaccines? What will happen with this?

M: Some people who are going through the experience with the vaccinations will have reactions to the vaccination and will, and have, already lost their lives. And yet we emphasize and like to remove the word lost because it is their time to transition. And so, part of their exit point had to do with a collective sacrifice which happened to transpire through the use of the vaccine. There will be some that will experience medical issues with inflammation, also with problems within organs that may not show for two to five years in time. And again, this has to do with their experience because what we have noted is that **the vaccine as anything else that is put into the body has all to do with the belief system and karmic agreement that takes place for each individual.**

S: Tell me more.

M: There are many sides to this coin and many different ways that this could be looked at. And although one could see a dark, more nefarious purpose to this agenda, this was a planned event, but we would say that all shades of dark are still part of the light. And we will say that there is always a purpose to each stage of it.

S: Will there be advancements from the side effects of these vaccines as there was in Atlantis?

M: There may be some who through what you would call side-effects will also have what you would call advancements or even new abilities. There will also be many children who will be born with differences in their vibration that will supersede the vaccine and this vibration will overcome any effect of the vaccine. But we will also say that there will be some that will come in with an effect of the vaccine and that will lead to studies because of these effects. This will also lead to medical discoveries when it comes to new assistance for some illnesses.

S: So, there will always be a benefit to everything.

M: Yes. Everything in the Universe.

S: Is there anything you could tell me about a being named Toth, or Three as he was called?

M: Yes, I feel that it is wrong to call this being a him or her, but rather both. And this being has come many times, but I feel that you are interested in when it came after Atlantis, correct?

S: Yes, why did he come?

M: Thoth/ Three is the writer of light. He is the carrier of information that was put down on the emerald tablets. Three holds the true scripture and it is protected information.

S: Why? Why is it protected information?

M: Because it holds the truth of our being, the truth of our eternalness, and of how we bring that eternalness into the physical body and ground that into the Earth.

S: How do we do that?

M: By connecting with the ancient part of ourselves, the original part of ourselves.

S: Where does this original part come from?

M: It comes from the creator but each one of us has the connection to what some would describe as the goddess or goddesses through Egyptian mythology. We call it truth. Many were practicing ancient agreements in Egypt.

S: Was Thoth a physical being?

M: He was a non-physical being.

S: Where did the writing come from?

M: There were lights that were coming down from the sky. He is part of that light, and he comes through many people and speaks through many people.

S: So, these scriptures hold the ancient truth? Is there a message that he would like to tell people?

M: All truth will be revealed in time. There will be a revealing of information that has been kept from humanity for many, many, generations.

S: When will this information be revealed?

M: We are in the decade of when it will be revealed.

S: Can it be revealed now? Could you tell me what this information is?

M: The information that can be revealed is that we are a fractal of the creator. Not as a totality of a being, but as a consciousness and that consciousness does not judge wrong or right but responds to the information that is believed and produced from each and every being. And over time, those on the Earth were persuaded into a belief that they were not in control of their own consciousness and decisions. So therefore, they looked outside of themselves for leadership and decisions. **And the truth comes from the individual understanding that they are the creator themselves, that they are a fractal of that consciousness, and so therefore have the power to be able to create from their own mind and frequency of the heart. The spiritual heart has its own vibration and its own existence just as much as the physical heart has its own existence.**

S: *They were practicing this in Egypt?*

M: Yes. Thoth spoke to these humans about these things.

S: *And this was hidden?*

M: Yes. After Atlantis and before the Ice age there was an opportunity for this information to come out and there were several opportunities that took place to have humanity be able to collectively step into power. This is a basic version.

S: *Is there another version? A not so basic one?*

M: Thoth lived for a very long time and worked to instill specific beings with information and helped them to learn about the power within themselves, to help them remember who they really were. The information that was hidden was not lost but hidden.

S: *Where was it hidden?*

M: In the Sphinx.

S: *Could you tell me what information is in the Sphinx? Is it beneficial to release some of the information?*
M: Some of it we can't release at this time. But what I can say is that we have technology and information, encoded technology, within the Sphinx that will be revealed. There are locations beneath the Sphinx, beneath the ground and around the pyramids that will rise when the collective reaches a certain consciousness. They will rise up.

S: *Will they physically rise?*

M: Yes, a crumbling effect will take place that will allow this information to physically rise. And this information that we share is just a primitive version, and what we are allowed to share at this time. **But what you need to understand is that our true history comes from the stars. Even the angels that you see in the bible come from the stars.**

S: *Could you tell me who am I speaking with?*

M: We are a team of beings; we are a part of Mary's guidance system. You could call us her higher self.
S: What kind of advice would you like to give humanity as we go through this chaotic time?

M: We see this as such an opportunity for change, and as chaotic as this is for many of you, which we can see, and feel, we would recommend that each one of you reach deep inside your heart and ask yourself "what do I believe," "what is most important for me," "what do I fixate on that isn't so important anymore," "what do I stand up for." And understanding this, we say focus on what you feel is right and not what you feel is wrong with your neighbor.

S: Is there anything that you could say about the divide amongst humans right now?

M: There is going to be a change in the way that government is viewed, is run.

S: Will this change happen soon?

M: There is a possibility that the government will change within two years. (This is August 2021)

S: Will the vaccine passports be implemented all over the world?

M: No. There will be a difference between law and what you would describe as mandate. And many will see mandate as law. There will be those that choose to not participate in the vaccine passport and there are ways that they will be able to focus their energy so that they are able to create a reality within a reality. The vaccine passport will be implemented as a permanent fixture for some, but not a law for others, and for some it will not affect them at all.

S: So, is it possible for a person to not participate because of what they focus on?

M: Yes, the collective reality is gaining momentum. So, to be able to see some of these potential realities is because of the collective reality. As the next two years go forward there are many who will have adjustments to their consciousness even though there will be some that will not awaken, some that had not intended to in this lifetime, and some by choice. But the ones that will awaken will be enough to be able to help create a reality that will bypass what would have been inevitable for the collective to experience.

S: Is it possible to create a reality?

M: It is possible to experience a reality based on what it is that you create. And so, if you are focusing your energy on what you believe to be true for you, regardless of what the collective reality is, you will be experiencing a reality that is so very different from one that is focused elsewhere. And the change in the dimensions will be very apparent in who and where one is focused at one time.
S: Tell me more.

M: How we would explain it is that one could be focused on a reality based on fear whereas another could be focused on another reality based on love. From a higher perspective as they do that, they create that experience for themselves, and both could be looking at the very same thing and experience something very different.

S: Is it possible to move into a different dimension right now? I've heard there is a lot of energy on the planet right now. If you can move into a different dimension, how do you do that?

M: Through your focus, but humans don't understand that they are moving into different dimensions all day every day. There is a moment to moment jumping that occurs. This is where you experience things like "I put this thing down on the counter, I come back, and it's gone and there's no one home." And they have just gone into a different reality. But to focus yourself into a different reality comes from a frequency of focus, a frequency of emotion, of intention, with the choosing of "what I would like to experience, what I would like to see." Even if what you would like to see is not apparent at that moment, choosing that frequency at any given situation and implementing that as your reaction will allow you to focus yourself into a different reality, especially at this time. As that frequency emits from you, from your light, your energy, your being, there is a structure that takes place, which if we were to explain this in the easiest way, is like an opening is created for you to enter into. And you may not realize or recognize anything different except that your reality is then bouncing back at you with the vibration and the frequency you were emitting.

S: So, you can do this?

M: This is happening quicker, with much faster momentum. Time is speeding up and so we remind you that each moment is like a film strip; it's like a flash. Each moment gives you the opportunity to be who it is that you want to be, and what it is that you would like to experience. And each moment is an imprint that you are putting into the computer system for the grid in the Earth. So, choose carefully.

S: What if you do something against your belief systems? Say you got the vaccine because of being pressured? Will you be, ok?

M: Just create a different experience; of course, you will be ok. What we would first say is that for all those who are using the virus, the vaccine, or any other type of way to exit the planet, there is no difference between whether it is a virus or any other way to exit. An exit point is simply that, an exit point. And so, if you are choosing to take the vaccine and die from it, we want you to understand that there is a timely choice there. And there would be a timeline where you would have the choice to exit in a different way. We also will say that not all that take the vaccine will die. Many will live and be perfectly fine. Side effects are personal and if a person does not need one to teach them something, they will not be a match to one. There will be many opportunities for those to go through illness, opportunities for those to experience the choice of going against what they feel is right for them, for the adversity in going against their own will, those are some of the greatest lessons.

S: Is there anything else about the ascension that seems important to share?

M: It's going as planned.

S: What is going as planned exactly?

M: Beings of many kinds that have incarnated on Earth at this time have done so, very bravely and although many are not aware, all have such a very important position, important job to play. To be able to raise the consciousness of humanity through this period affects the whole Universe. The importance of this happening at this time has been projected for billions of years and the times of exit that the planet has taken in the past has affected so many other systems. We have always known that there would be rejuvenation at this time. And therefore, that's why there has been so much help and trust from the other benevolent beings from the stars.

S: Why now, why is this happening now?

M: Many reasons. Part of it has to do with the coordinates of the Earth's placement, we will say the energy is right, the substance around the planet is very supportive for Earth to pass through this gate, this threshold. It is an exchange of one system of, we will say barrier or control, to a system of freedom. We could look at that in many ways, there are many different ways that we could explain that, but the easiest answer that we would give, is that now produces the very best fruit on the tree.

S: Tell me more.

M: This is the ascension, the consciousness evolution, the human evolution, the human and technology evolution, and the introduction of unseen technology. It is the biggest growth of evolution at this time.

S: Will humans know that this is happening? Will they be aware?

M: Eventually they will. There will be a time where humanity understands history, the history as it was truly written.

S: When do you see this happening?

M: The next ten years will be a great source of learning and expansion, but each person needs to understand the root source of all consciousness in the Universe in order to understand how you can use consciousness to see the future. All ETs go beyond the speed of light to go into more conscious dimensions. And the way that the ETs communicate are with thought and the consciousness field. Each being in the Universe is a blueprint of the totality of all consciousness. And once you understand this, you will ascend because you are actually the one with the power. This future is waiting for us as much as we are for it.

Similar information kept coming through in sessions with many different clients who did not know one another and had not heard this information before consciously. Below is another segment of a session that I feel is relevant to this. Wanda came in for a session and found herself tuning into what appeared to be a portal within the Sphinx. When she tuned into this, it appeared that there were beings waiting to communicate with us. This is the segment.

W: As I was just tuning into what appears to be a portal within the Sphinx, I feel a stream of consciousness that appears to have beings that wish to communicate.

S: Who are these beings and what do they wish to say?

W: They are from the Pleiades. They wish to talk.

S: What do they want to say?

W: They say that they wish that human beings would detach from this idea that they are not whole. They are always trying to become, when they already are. And so, they suffer, and they have pain, and they pretend to be less than they are. And that keeps them in a constant state of despair and suffering.

S: What advice would you like to give humans then?

W: To remember that you are God experiencing yourself. The first step is in remembering who you are, and what you came here to be, and not subscribing to anyone else's definition of who you are.

S: How does a person remember who they are?

W: By waking up. Humans live in a society where they are being put to sleep all the time due to the control and power structure which works better when everyone is asleep. And so, it is important to unplug from this machine to remember that you are lovable, to remember that nature is here for you, to remember that abundance is everywhere and that there is no lack.

S: Who am I speaking with?

W: You could call me whatever you wish.

S: How do you know Wanda exactly?

W: I am a version of Wanda, a higher consciousness. I am essentially her.

S: How are you a version of her? Are you also having a lifetime now as well?

W: I am a higher dimensional being. I have been having a lifetime for eons. But now my lifetime is whatever I choose it to be.

S: What do you choose to do?

W: I like to come here and help Wanda and guide her. I like to drop into the forest. It's beautiful to be here on Earth.

S: What do you do when you are in the forest?

W: Play, run, jump, and have fun. I love Earthly delights.

S: Do you have nature where you normally live?

W: Yes. I live in the Pleiades. It's very beautiful.

S: Could you tell me about it?

W: Yes. There are many of us higher dimensional beings here. It's full of love and very few problems and very few issues. We've mostly figured out the things that you struggle with here on Earth. But because of that, because there is a lack of mess, there is also a lack of polarization, and we like to sometimes have the dichotomy of polarization. We like to come to Earth and feel, and be messy, and be joyful, and have tears.

S: There is nature where you live? Could you tell me about it?

W: It's beautiful. It's different than Earth, but it is beautiful. Our sky is pink and purple. Our grass is not grass; our ground is not the same. Earth has oceans and many different biospheres, and the Pleiades do not have that. The Pleiades are magical to look at, it is beautiful. It would completely astound you. Conversely it is boring sometimes because it is always the same.

S: Do you feel bored?

W: I feel malaise. At this point in our evolution, it is very easy to be bored.

S: I thought it was blissful there always?

W: Blissful is not always exciting. Earth is exciting, because there is so much happening, and the pace is fast. Although the pace at which things actually occur in the Pleiades is much faster.

S: Tell me about that.

W: Earth is very dense in comparison. We can have what we want immediately. We have telepathy when we speak to one another from far distances. We do not have emotional turmoil. We have elevated from all of that.

S: How did you do that?

W: We have been working towards that for a very long time and in a very fast fashion. We have agreements amongst our beings to reach higher points of ascension and we are harmonious in our agreements. And so, we are working towards that goal at all times.

S: How did you get to that point in your evolution?

W: It is our collective agreement, and we just came there with that. We have always had this agreement and it is the basis of our society. Whereas the basis of the society on Earth is to muck around and figure things out. Human beings are very messy.

S: *Why?*

W: Well, that is their job. Their job is to be messy. There is no perfection in human beings. Their imperfection is their perfection. Their ability to feel, to emote, to connect is their gift and sometimes that becomes disastrous, sometimes that becomes messy, and most times it is very, very beautiful to observe.

S: *So, you observe humans?*

W: We do observe humans. We are guides to anyone who asks for our guidance.

S: *What can a human do with your guidance?*

W: They could channel our energy. They could channel our higher consciousness. They could allow us to be advisors for them. We walk amongst you daily. We live with you, and we enjoy Earth. We are you.

S: *Do you have any more advice for us?*

W: Humans could be happier if they stop arguing for their own limitations. Human beings have a habit of saying that they cannot, they are not allowed, they have no choices. And the truth is that they have everything available to them at all times. Look at a tree. There are so many leaves on that tree. The tree never says I wonder if all of these leaves will fall off, they just let the leaves fall and let the new leaves grow. That is an act of surrender and trust. And so human beings could take a lesson from the tree and let what's not for them fall away so something new can come. Remember that there is always abundance. This entire Universe is abundant.

CHAPTER 21: LOOKING FOR CHRISTIE

Jen and I met again for another session to take a closer look at the life review that Christie had in the in-between state. While Jen recounted this in depth look shocking details about this woman's life started to emerge.

S: What do you become aware of?

J: It's time to go over my life as Christie now with my guide.

S: As you go over your lifetime as Christie with your guide are there any details about that life that you notice or that seems important?

J: As I focus over that life, I see it all more clearly, like watching a movie. I see that I lived on a smaller street that has many brownstones all piled up next to each other, but they're only about two stories high; they're not very tall. It looks like it's in a quiet neighborhood, like maybe a suburb, not directly in the center of Manhattan. There are several children that live there with my friend's mom and I, they are all in their teenage years. It was a very full house. It looks like the neighborhood is also filled with many families. It feels very much like I lived somewhere between Queens or Brooklyn. But if I were to look outside of the house, I can clearly see a street sign. I lived on Oak Street!

S: Is there anything about the mental hospital that looks important?

J: I see it; it says Bellevue! It's the Bellevue mental hospital in New York City. I see that it was 1978 when I passed because I can see the date on a newspaper. I must have seen this paper after my death because it clearly says July 1978.

S: When you were taken to the mental hospital around Christmas time, how long do you feel that you stayed there before you threw yourself off the bridge?

J: About two, maybe three months at the most.

S: After you jumped off the bridge was there any record of that in the papers?

J: I'm looking from this perspective, but I don't see anything. I think they tried to cover it up as much as possible because they didn't want the knowledge getting out that their inmates could escape. They didn't want people to think that a dangerous person could've been running around on the streets. It looks like I was just counted as another Jane Doe until my mother was notified that I went missing from the hospital.

S: *How did she react?*

J: She looks devastated. She looks like everything she had ever done wrong in her entire life with me came back and hit her in the face.

S: *If you go into her house, does she have any mail laying around with her name on it?*

J: I see piles and piles of mail. It looks like she becomes a hoarder. Her stuff is dirty, everything has been piled up on top of each other. Mail and junk are just everywhere. Looking at her mail I believe her name was Matty or Matilda.

S: *Can you see any letters with her address on it?*

J: I see what looks like twenty-six Elizabeth Street. There is a letter next to the number, but I can't see that clearly. She lives on the lower east side of Manhattan and that is also where I was born. It's amazing how much I can see from this perspective! It seems that she lives up a flight of stairs. It's very hot and very stuffy there. There aren't a lot a lot of windows and you can smell her apartment before you get to it. She has become a hoarder in the aftermath of my death. She hoards things around her to protect herself from the emotions of what she had done to me, of what she drove me to do in the absence of her mothering. She spends the rest of her life feeling this way, and it looks like she dies alone, and no one knows that she had died for quite a few weeks. She kills herself surrounding herself with all this stuff to replace me, wishing she had done things differently.

S: *Anything else you notice about this?*

J: We agreed to not come back together this time. This was not something that would serve either one of us, and we chose to not be together again in this life I live as Jen. Oh my gosh! (gasp) I think she saw me as a child! We saw each other, I'm just realizing this now!

S: *Tell me more.*

J: I'm seeing that in this current life as Jen that I saw an older woman walking past me when I was in a stroller in Manhattan, and I remember that we recognized each other for a brief moment. It was very strange! But I understand this memory now, and who this woman is. That was my mother from that life as Christie! I was very little, maybe two at the absolute most in this stroller.

S: *What was it like when you saw each other?*

J: She was walking by, and we looked at each other and she knew!

S: *Do we always meet people that were in our lifetimes before?*

J: We try to, especially for the ones we want to, and we avoid the ones we would like to avoid in order to accomplish certain goals in each lifetime. It's not always successful, sometimes you cannot help but have the other's free will interfere with your own and other times you simply miss the opportunity.

S: Tell me more about when you saw your previous mother in this current life as Jen.

J: It feels like a slap in the face for her at first because we don't know each other, but she knows it's me.

S: How does she know it's you?

J: She can feel it, she can sense it. She senses my spirit. She senses that something within me is part of her. There is a connection that we have and even though in that lifetime as Christie it was very bad between the two of us, she knows that I am the soul of Christie, the child that she held in her arms after she gave birth to me.

S: What does she do after she sees you there?

J: We are in downtown around the Wall Street area, and I see that there are large, big steps of granite all around us. I think she was sitting on the steps, smoking a cigarette, and looking around when I passed by in the stroller. And as I passed by her, I turned, and I looked up and made eye contact with her. It lasted for what felt like forever, and I could see it in her eyes. I knew it was her, but I didn't know who she was at the time. Afterwards it looks like she sat there crying. And she walked after that to the water, her hands shaking as she chain-smokes. She's very upset. She thinks about all the things that she could've done differently and it's just too late for that.

S: Where does she walk?

J: She walks to where I left that life, the Brooklyn bridge. She spends the day mourning me and the loss of our relationship, and all the things that she had done wrong.

S: When you were living with your friend's family, is there anything else about that that seems interesting?

J: I'm not sure it was a friend. It might've been a boyfriend that I lived with. He wasn't someone I was ever in love with though, just a form of protection to help me.

S: Tell me about this boyfriend?

J: I don't feel like we were a good match for each other. He was not very interesting, but he was not a hurtful person either. I have trouble seeing him.

S: Did you stay in the same room as this boyfriend in your friend's house?

J: We had different rooms. I stayed downstairs in the basement, and he was upstairs. It was a strange relationship; he had asked me out so many times, but I wasn't interested. He was my only friend at school for a long time. He was infatuated with me, but I continuously told him that I just wanted to be friends. I wasn't interested in dating anyone.

S: How did you end up moving in with him?

J: I had to leave my mother's home. I had to leave because it was too abusive there. Her husband was hurting us every day. He was hurting us and drinking away all of our money. It was unbearable and it feels like there was a day where just everything exploded, and I took what I could take, and I left. I didn't know where I was going or what I was going to do, but I remember this friend saw me in front of this corner store, and he saw me crying and upset. He pulled me aside and told me that he understood what was going on and offered to take me to his house where I could spend the night. He said that I could stay there on the couch and that his mother would make me dinner. He said it wasn't safe for me to be wandering around. Our neighborhoods are very dirty. They look like a place where there are cars that are burnt out and just piled up underneath the highways, and there's just so much trash. Wherever there's not a house or a building there is just trash piled up in what looks like landfills everywhere. It feels very violent there as well; it was true that that area was just very unsafe.

S: Is this your neighborhood?

J: This is the lower east side. He was still going to school that day. He lived over there for many years, but his parents divorced, and he finally moved to Brooklyn with his mother and siblings. And that is where his house was. We took the bus there; I think we walked over the bridge together and then took the bus ride from there, and it was about fifteen minutes to get there by bus.

S: What happened when you got there?

J: His mother was kind but was very distracted by all the people and children she had in the house. She was the parental guidance for all of them and there seems to be about five or six kids there. She was constantly distracted and never really focused on you entirely, but she could listen to what you were saying and answer you but could also still be cooking dinner at the same time. She was a very busy multitasker. So, you never really felt like you were sitting there getting one on one time with her. But that was fine because we got along, but we weren't very close. And it was better that we just had this understanding between the two of us that I would start working and I was allowed to live in the basement. I think I moved in with them just a few weeks after my graduation.

S: After you got a job, did you still stay there?

J: I did. I stayed there for a while, not a very long time. My friend introduced me to everyone as his girlfriend even though I wasn't, and I quickly pointed out to everyone that we were just friends. They thought it was humorous but over time he just wore away at me, and I did become his girlfriend. I was never really interested in him, he was just so persistent, and I had nowhere else I could go.

S: What happened when he learned that you were in the mental institution?

J: He never reached out or came to help me. I think he believed what he had heard about me, that

I was suffering from female hysteria and didn't think to question it.

S: Do you get a sense if there were any pictures taken of you?

J: Yes, there were. He had pictures of us, he looks very happy in them.

S: Can you look and see where you might find one of these pictures of you?

J: There are pictures of us, and from what I see, there are pictures of me as a baby shoved in boxes in storage units that no one would recognize because they are no longer the property of people who would have remembered me. They have been piled away and pushed away.

S: Will anyone ever find a picture of you as Christie?

J: After people read this and understand and see her for who she is, they will be able to envision her as I remember her. It's possible that someone may be able to come across pictures of her by chance. There's one picture of us where he has his arm bent around me and he looks so proud of himself, and I look like I've been captured. I'm wearing a dark yellow and white cream outfit with a daisy embroidered on it in this picture.

CHAPTER 22: THREE, AND THE SECRETS OF THE SPHINX

In the Spring of 2021, Jen left the Florida Keys to move to Hawaii to reunite with her lost civilization of Lemuria as best as she could. As sad as I was to not be able to work as much as we were, I was happy that she was able to finally move back to what she considered her home. In my own past life regression in which I learned of my previous incarnation in Atlantis as a judge, I had wanted to free Jen, to help her, and to allow her to go back home, only her home had been destroyed along with her family and everyone she loved so much. Through our series of regressions, we learned that Jen's daughter who had passed in the cataclysm that destroyed Lemuria had reincarnated as her daughter again in this current life. And so, Jen took her family and moved back to Hawaii, moving back to the closest place to where Lemuria would have been. I'm sure the energy could still be felt there, and I smiled at the thought of her taking her daughter back there as well. I, on the other hand, still felt as if I had to stay close to the old energy of Atlantis in the Keys; my work here doesn't feel done yet. I had been looking for another willing subject, and I thought about a session that I had had a year ago with a client named Fred. Fred had come in for a session to heal a rare form of arthritis which had been diagnosed as incurable. In Fred's session he realized that he had been contacted by extra-terrestrials since childhood and his session was very surprising, healing and enlightening for him. His healing from his QHHT session surprised everyone including his doctors. Fred had never read a Dolores Cannon book, had no previous knowledge of past life regression, or spiritual knowledge and so I felt that Fred would be an excellent subject. I prefer subjects who do not have any previous conscious knowledge when working with them in order to validate and trust the information that I receive. I feel that it is important for the integrity of this work. So, I asked Fred if he would like to delve further into the information that we were receiving and if he would like to come back for another session. Here is my next session with Fred.

S: *What do you become aware of?*

F: I woke up to a loud bang and realized that the noise was only in my head, if that makes sense. I felt this loud popping in my ears as I felt myself floating up through the ceiling to a ship, and it was a strange feeling as I moved up past the ceiling. It's as if just a part of me feels the texture of the ceiling. The ship has five lights on the bottom and the color of the ship looks like it's a brownish color. I feel the wind, it feels very surreal and nice as I go up. Then when I get into the ship, it's just white and light. Everything looks like it's made of a pulsing light. It almost looks as if the ship is breathing. I feel that the ship itself has a consciousness.

S: *Tell me more.*

F: The bottom of the ship looks like the inside of a fan, where it looks like it sucks energy up through the bottom and uses that energy through the fan and propels it in different directions. There is something about the way the propeller underneath it works that lifts and pulls from a force that is tapped into. Now I'm on a table and the little greys are all around me, trying to ask me questions through my mind. They have an amazing ability to bounce my emotions and thoughts back to myself as if they were the ones coming up with them; they are sweet in their approach with me. The bigger ones are the ones that get close to me.

S: What is happening?

F: I'm on a table. It feels cold and it feels like a doctor's office visit almost, but these beings get very close to my face. Their eyes, it looks like they contain swirling galaxies in their eyes. They are examining me, and they are pointing to my leg because they put something in there.

S: Tell me more. Why do they get so close to you?

F: They're just trying to save their race. They have been around a long time, but for some reason I know them, but I knew a different them in a different lifetime. This was after there was a technological ascension.

S: Tell me more about that?

F: They would do things to prolong life for themselves and they realize now that that was a mistake. They almost erased their feelings. Now they don't have reproduction capabilities because there were so many of them that they ended up becoming sterile. They have mostly robotic bodies now because they made parts for themselves to be able to survive.

S: They advanced but couldn't breed anymore?

F: They don't have the same spark that we have. They are after our spark and that's why people are afraid of them. People think they are going to steal our spark.

S: Are they?

F: No, this is just an agreement. I came from this planet. I used to be one of these beings! I'm just in this human body now for this life.

S: Where are they from?

F: It looks like a planet that has already reached the end of its life. It used to look different, it used to look similar to Earth, but just a little different. It has these...I guess you would call them spires that I can go into. Going into the spires feels very crackly and loud like a tornado of electricity. It feels nice.

S: Tell me more.

F: I see things in here, there is information in here.

S: *What type on information?*

F: The history of this planet is in there. It stores everything that has happened to us and our civilization.

S: *Is there anything interesting about the information that you notice?*

F: Just like every planet that we have seeded, we start from nothing and evolve. It's really interesting because I see information about the volcanos and mountains on Earth for some reason.

S: *What kind of information about volcanos and mountains do you see?*

F: Volcanos and mountains contain a very deep energetic source of something we have yet to tap into that naturally resonates from these large mountains, especially ones that have the ability to produce this kind of heat energy.

S: *What do you mean exactly?*

F: The heat energy functions as a fuel source. The mountains and volcanos resonate this high frequency heat energy that pulsates out because of this heat and this energy that's created within this opening from the Earth. It's easy for other beings to connect to this energy, but humans have yet to understand it. **It powers a lot of these ships that they travel on.** It is like a super powered solar energy, the equivalent of being able to tap into an energy from a natural resource. It is a superpowered version of it that could power a ship forever.

S: *How does it work? How does it power the ship?*

F: It has a natural kind of ripple effect that comes out of the mountain or volcano and almost like if you drop something in the water and it ripples out. It's like that in that it just naturally pulsates out from the volcano or opening of a mountain. Beings just need to tune the receptors in their devices to this energy and it literally just absorbs into these. This is like the same way you put your phone on one of the charging pads and it charges your phone without being connected to something. It has this attraction and absorption.

S: *Is this why people see so many ships around volcanos?*

F: It is one of the reasons

S: *Can a human use this energy?*

F: They can, but humans haven't tapped into how to do this yet. There are many who have tried and many who have failed.

S: *How do you do it? How does a human tap into the energy?*

F: We don't have the right devices to use it just yet. It is a propulsion energy. It radiates outwards and it's very strong, and you can't see it, but it looks like rings of light lilac-colored energy that comes out from the Earth.

S: Tell me more.

F: The energy that comes from the mountains and volcanos is also connected to the ley lines that were used to travel throughout the Earth.

S: So, the ley lines connect to the volcanoes?

F: Yes. There is a very intricate system of grids on the Earth and these mountains and volcanos are power sources.

S: Is there anything that happens with the energy when the volcano erupts?

F: Yes. That is part of Earth's changes and patterns and sometimes things need to be expelled in order to produce a purer form of energy. The impure energy is expelled so that new growth can be made. Many beings from all over the Universe use this energy.

S: Who are these beings exactly?

F: Beings from all over, many beautiful light beings. Their future is our future. And with cooperation and comradery we can prevent possible disasters because they have the technology to undo all the things that we've done to our world, and we in turn have the vessels which are useful to them to try to continue as a species.

S: How do they use our vessels exactly?

F: Through genetic manipulation. Every human alive has DNA which is altered to allow a signal from a separate place to come in. So, you don't just have your soul energy coming in, you have your Earth energy, a star person energy, a grey energy. You might have these different essences in one, but these energies still get to experience a full life. They are having their experiences, but we are now their new forefathers even though they are ours.

S: So, it's like a figure Eight? It never starts or ends? So, we are their future, and they are ours?

F: Yes, and they are trying to make babies. They make hybrid babies in tubes. Some of them can't live in Earth's atmosphere and require visits from the mothers. The mothers who are taken from Earth in their sleep are brought to the birthing places and the centers where the kids are to have relationships, even if they don't remember it.

S: Is there anything about that they want us to know?

F: They are just trying to survive. They feel bad for everything they have done to their people and for leading them to where they are.

S: *Why do they feel bad? What did they do that they wish they didn't?*

F: They feel bad for abandoning hope and going too far with their technology. They realize the mistake of being afraid of death to the point where they kept themselves alive for millennia through technology and things like that.

S: *So, they feel that they went wrong by abandoning hope and moving on with too much technology?*

F: Yes, they abandoned hope and just went into the science world instead of allowing themselves to naturally live or die. They instead tried through their technology to live forever. And they don't emote these things to you necessarily, when you meet them; they seem very cold, very methodical. But by abandoning their hope it led them to a dark place, and they are trying to save themselves and teach us what not to do at the same time.

S: *What do they want to teach us exactly?*

F: That you can live forever but that comes with a price. The natural way of things is to die when it's your time. It's also nice to evolve in ways that don't put you in situations that they were faced with where you have to leave your planet and not have a place to go back to. They have lived amongst the stars for countless millennia to where they no longer even look the same.

S: *Why did they have to leave their planet?*

F: It ran dry, they sucked it dry. Their technology, advancements, mining... all that stuff led to them just eventually having a husk of a planet.

S: *What did they used to look like?*

F: They used to look a lot like us. As you would say they are us in the future, but they were taller before they developed the darker skin and strange complexion.

S: *How did they get the darker skin and strange complexion?*

F: By evolving yourself past the point of needing to eat. When you don't eat food, then you don't use your mouth. The size of their eyes adapted to the darkness since they are out in space. Slow evolution allowed their bones to separate and become further apart and longer limbed because there is less gravity in space. This is just an evolutionary process over millions of years for them. They are what we would look like after millions of years in space.

S: *So why would they want to keep reproducing?*

F: They want to reel it back a little by creating hybrid children so that they can come into a physical body on this Earth.

S: So eventually they will live amongst us on this Earth?

F: They are already here, and the hybrids of all different races are here as well.

S: And that is so that the different beings can inhabit the Earth?

F: Yes, so they can experience the school of ascension.

S: Why is this called the school of ascension?

F: The Earth is like a school for souls. You can complete the grade, some people skip a grade, but the way it's set up is unless you learn your lessons you just keep repeating them. You have to move up the ladder to graduate, to ascend. So, you have to become a more enlightened being to move up to the fifth dimension, sixth dimension, etc. You have to be pure in understanding. Earth is where you come to learn all that, because when you start out, you're just a blank slate. You're actually pure light when you get here. And then Earth takes ahold of you and throws everything at you from colds to bullies, to bills… everything and the whole trick is to keep that innocence and the light lit the whole time.

S: How do you do that?

F: It's very simple. Have compassion and do what you love to do. And if you keep doing that every day you will move up, and there are a lot of people that have moved up, and gone on, and graduated this school. After which, a lot of them come back.

S: Tell me more about that?

F: Deity level beings from stories of old, still come down into a physical form here and forget everything. This is really strange, but there is someone, or what feels like a being, who wishes to speak, to share more information. Information about the Sphinx?

S: A being wants to share information about the Sphinx? What does this being wish to say?

F: (Laugh) It just says it will answer your questions now.

S: What do you want to tell me about the Sphinx?

F: Do you have questions for us?

S: Yes. Ok, I have several questions. Are there holes within the Sphinx, and, if so, what are they used for?

F: There are several holes within the Sphinx that have to do with the stars and the absorption of the energy from the sun. The light can enter inside through these holes and is able to create energy and vortexes. They are used for energy and power and were designed by your ancestors, your star friends and family. There are codes through vibration, information, and messages within the Sphinx. There are crystals inside as well.

S: *Why are there crystals within the Sphinx?*

F: They are set up in the form of a grid from the very earliest times during Atlantis when they were hidden there. This grid is for communication and holding information.

S: *So, the holes within the Sphinx have to do with the stars, light and create energy and vortexes?*

F: Yes, just like electricity creates power; they create power that can be tapped into.

S: *How do you tap into this power?*

F: Through the right information, the right circumstances, and with an alignment of solar systems. A human being that would be able to tap into this would need some instruction and information that is located within the Sphinx.

S: *How can a person find this and use this?*

F: We believe, to answer the question in the way that you are wanting the answer, that this has to do with the timing, the alignment, and to be able to tap into this energy information. For the instruction does not come through a specific manual but it is held within the vibrations of the crystals, the information that is there. Some of this will be released as we go forward.

S: *When do you mean?*

F: As the planet goes forward there will be some recognition of your history, the history you have been taught compared to the history that is your truth. And as that is discovered new vortexes will open that give access to technology and information that is connected to our true past and projects, which in turn will create your new future.

S: *This will happen once humans understand true history? How will they understand true history; what will happen for this history to come out?*

F: There is a maturity that is taking place through the collective on Earth, and as people develop their ability to communicate with those that are not known to be on Earth, then through them this information will become known.

S: *How will it become known? Will humans spread this information and share it? Or will beings share this?*

F: There will be beings that will communicate with those on Earth. It will appear to many to look like rumor, it will start out as rumor. It will start out as unsure. We see that there may be some false starts where some things are created that are not actually true, and behind that the truth will be released. We see this as being complementary to the change in government systems on Earth. And we do see that the Sphinx will have accessible parts that were not seen as accessible before at this time.

S: What parts will be accessible?

F: Entrances. One is at the back; one is at the foot.

S: What will happen when a person enters the Sphinx?

F: When humanity has reached a level of existence where this is possible, it would still depend on the person and the vibration that the person exists within. A person of a vibration that aligns with the Sphinx would find themselves in an environment where they can charge themselves, one that will allow them to connect to other locations and has the potential to transport consciousness.

S: Could you tell me more about that?

F: There are many different things that people have learned such as connecting their crystals to copper or connecting portals to energy to create gateways on Earth. We see that within the Sphinx is a contained gateway. The Sphinx is from your star ancestors and star family. It is created like a temple, like a place to come together to be able to have a concentrated amount of energy so that one may transport themselves to different locations.

S: Why was the face changed from the face of a jungle cat to one of a pharaoh?

F: This was a discrepancy of power. This was a time when man was starting to take ownership of power in a different way. We would know this as the suppression of the feminine. This was when the human started to separate more from the source, and within that there was treason. There was backstabbing, a need to take control of others. A feeling of I will be the leader, you will follow. This is what has led to thousands of years of, what some call, the Piscean age of power and greed. This is what our world has known in the third dimension, a world of corporations and climbing the corporate ladder. And so, as there are many symbols in the world, this began as a symbol. This was putting the face of the man that considered himself the leader, the face of the corporation, not the face of the originator.

S: How did they put this face on the Sphinx?

F: There was technology that they had from an earlier time and that technology was given to them.

S: Was there a second Sphinx?

F: Yes, the feminine version of the Sphinx is buried and in pieces now, but it is located close to the original one. The masculine and feminine have always been the polarity that created balance. The feminine will rise, is rising. The feminine that some consider crumbled may not be physically what we can see with our eyes at this time, but as the feminine rises on Earth, these pieces of the feminine version of the second Sphinx will rise from the ground.

S: *Will people be aware of the second Sphinx when this rising occurs?*

F: Very much so. The feminine has always been there. She has always been a quiet and silent partner, but now she roars.

S: *Why are there underground tunnels under the Sphinx?*

F: We see them as connectors that allow one to travel from one place to another, but there are also many dead ends.

S: *Why are there dead ends?*

F: To confuse the wrong people from entering and to throw off anyone that shouldn't be there. There are some items that are protected. Some of them are red crystals, but the items are very powerful and so must be hidden at this time.

S: *What is written on the Sphinx?*

F: The story of two beings.

S: *Who put this story there?*

F: The ancestors.

S: *What is the message that this story tells?*

F: It is the foretelling of what is ahead, of what will come back, of how it is our destiny to seed this planet. It is the story of eternal life, revival and cycles. The story is actually meant to protect this information from the wrong hands. This story carries information about history in its true form.

S: *What kind of history?*

F: Creation. The origin of Earth. Earth is a planet that was created with help from beings of the stars. There are many that are not prepared to hear this.

S: *Why?*

F: The truth will scare many because it will be so contrasting to what they have believed. Some it will excite, and this is some of the truth that we speak of that will come across as a rumor before it is known as truth.

S: *Is there anything else you would like humanity to understand now?*

F: The Universes, the Creator, all beings in existence, they are from one source.

S: Tell me more.

F: We see this as a cell. There is one huge cell, which is a Universe, with many Universes within. There are what we would call Gods, Goddesses, and many Earths. All of these come from the same place, the same source.

S: Tell me more.

F: This is not the first Earth, and soon humans will understand that the hidden cities that are under the sea, the lost cities, are not fairy tales.

S: I wrote about that in my previous book.

F: Yes, you are able to tap into this information, and there are many versions of your books, and although this version of this book is being written now, it has had to be changed slightly based on what is necessary for all those on Earth to hear at this time.

S: Is there anything else that you would like humans to hear at this time?

F: Yes. Have no fear, there are still steps to be walked through that may create fear. There is an eternal world that does not run by a clock that is working its way into this new reality. This world was predicted many times to come to an end. And we say this world is coming to an end as we know it, but we are birthing a new World. And like labor when a child is born, the female will go through labor pains. There is excitement knowing what is about to come into the world. And although those labor pains are uncomfortable, we don't know how long it will go, we don't know how long the labor will be, but we know it will come to an end soon. We know that it won't go on this way forever. And when it comes, and that child enters the world, there is a sense of euphoria and a sense of excitement and a looking back at all we have been through. And so, we say as this new World is being birthed, to hold on tight, for we are almost there.

S: Was sound used in the Sphinx?

F: Yes. Sound frequency and light is the carrier of information. There are codes that carry information back and forth from one's family in the stars to those on Earth. These messages carry frequencies for healing, for wisdom, for expansion of understanding, for mystical teaching and many purposes.

S: What happened to the Sphinx during the Ice Age?

F: We see it as being buried; we see it as having corrosion around it. It was covered in sand. But the power has always been there, and the power of the Sphinx has never been lost.

S: Why is there sand in Egypt?

F: There was once water, and many went to higher ground because that area where the Sphinx is located was once under water at one time. The pyramids were created many thousands of years after the Sphinx and are connected and can work individually as well as work together. They also can work with other elements around the world. There are other structures that have this same sacred power that can light up a grid on the Earth creating a gateway for travel.

S: *What do you mean by a gateway for travel exactly?*

F: We think the best way to explain it is like creating a highway that travels through dimensions, a pathway.

S: *Is the information that I have so far for this book correct? Or is there anything that I need to change?*

F: Since it has been a collective effort to get this information out, we would say that this is what we have wanted. More will be released in time. There are teachings of how we structure our reality.

S: *How do we structure our reality?*

F: Through the power of the mind using vibration and energy, through connection of the third eye and the pineal gland and connecting eye to eye between people. How this was done, how the buildings were able to connect from point to point is representative of the human body and how it connects from point to point. The top of the pyramid is the top of the crown, the pineal gland. That connects from point to point, from being to being. This creates a sacred energy which can manifest, can move, can bring forward objects buried in the ground. We can see things moving when they connect into this energy grid. We can see things coming up from the sand, coming to light. We can see large objects moving. We can see things begin that the human body can't do without the power of the mind.

S: *Tell me more.*

F: This type of power allows humans to be able to defy gravity, not only with their own weight, but with objects that would be impossible for their mass to move or lift.

S: *What can a human do with this information?*

F: When that power is directed, when it is connected in with one, with two with three beings much can be accomplished. They can build realities from within themselves.

S: *So, cocreation is important?*

F: Yes. Build within yourself. Raise the strength of your focused intention and frequency within yourself. And learn to sit and connect in with others. Focus together. Many beings will have different attributes or qualities that may differ from one another, but when coming together it is like a recipe. When it works together it makes the perfect meal, the perfect baked good.

S: Tell me more.

F: With focused belief and with power, many can come together and create great change, create movement, move mountains. And we mean that on literal terms. It is the intention of the new World.

S: Are there any other secrets within the Sphinx?

F: There is more than one level to it. There are lower chambers within, almost like quarters of rest, temples, places of prayer.

S: What are the purposes of those different levels?

F: The were used for healing.

S: Do you have to go inside the Sphinx to experience the healing?

F: A human can tap into this through belief or visualization. We see many standing around the Sphinx holding hands. But the healing would depend on their individual frequencies. So, they would have to match to this healing frequency.

S: Is there anything else that you would like to share?

F: There are scrolls within the Sphinx, containers of information that have been placed there until the time comes when they will be used. They are instructions, but they would not be understood at this time. They are light codes. At one point they were placed there in case the plan did not get carried out. The scrolls are not as important now because the Earth is ascending. So, there is no worry for failure. We didn't know this at the time when we placed these light codes within these scrolls. The light codes were also left in different spots on the Earth that are a part of the grid. It was part of the overall plan to help humanity to ascend. However, they have already done their job because the Earth is ascending. It is happening. The Sphinx was used to create a higher frequency because of the formation of the geometry on the surface of the Earth where it is placed. It creates a direct channel to the center of the Earth as well and elevates the frequency. It is designed to draw out and bring in light to the Earth. There is a pyramid shape and labyrinth under the Sphinx.

S: Why is there a labyrinth under the Sphinx?

F: There is a very elaborate labyrinth underneath, but very deep, closer to the center. There are several purposes. It connects the inner Earth consciousness, the communities within the inner Earth to the different pockets within the Earth like veins, and it helps to distribute the light. It is a key in the Earths' ascension. It is a way for the inner Earth beings and the humans on the surface to exchange energy and information.

S: How?

F: These tunnels help to deliver the light from the core of the Earth to the surface. This will be important as the new Earth communities are forming because there will be a lot more communication between the inner Earth communities and those on the surface. There will be more conscious communication in the future.

S: If a person goes to the Sphinx, is there anything that they could do to communicate with the Sphinx?

F: You could channel the Sphinx's consciousness to see what it has to say.

S: Could we see what it has to say now? Could I speak with the Sphinx?

F: Yes, you can.

S: Do you think about things? (Question to the Sphinx)

F: I do not think; I am.

S: Do you have a personality?

F: Yes, one could say that. I am more feminine in that I am in a sense a passive energy. I am part light, not by doing or by thinking, but by being.

S: What is your purpose in this existence?

F: I am a beacon of light on Earth, one of many.

S: How has this experience on Earth been for you?

F: It has been truly splendid to be here on Earth all this time, to be here and to witness evolution unfolding.

S: If you were to give a message to humanity, what would you say?

F: I am you, and you are me, we are the same.

S: So, essentially humans are the Sphinx?

F: Yes, we are the same consciousness.

S: Is there anything else that you would like to say?

F: To forget is only temporary. It's only a fraction of a moment that you forget. Remembering is what you came here for. Suffering can feel so deep and so great, but this is only because you have forgotten. It feels like much time or eons pass, but suffering is really just a blink of an eye. But bliss is what you feel and experience most of the time. Suffering is very short so don't feel weary, everything is well. I promise you that everything is well.

S: What happens to you during Earth's ascension?

F: I remain here simply as a presence and a reminder for you. There are many clues that have been placed here on Earth. I am one of those, to help the human remember what their truth is and where they are from, to help with the amnesia that you have created for yourselves. And at the same time, you have also created and left clues so that you could remember as I am one of those clues.

S: Do you have any other messages for humanity?

F: There will be more and more light accumulating on Earth and the frequency will continue to rise. So, you can prepare yourself for this light by knowing who you are. Let go of the belief that you are just a fragile human, for you are me, you are beingness and consciousness. That's what you are. That is all. We will bring back the previous conduit. Goodbye.

S: (Asking Fred) Is there anything else about the Sphinx that is important, or did I ask everything already?

F: This whole Universe, including the Sphinx is like a hologram with shimmering reflections of you in there. In a hologram you can break it into two pieces, shine a light on each side and it will still have a whole image on both sides even if it was broken. And that original piece was the source, source energy. We're all little pieces of that, splintered off and shattered all across existences, levels, dimensions, dew drops…everything…everywhere. But every single sliver has the blueprint of the whole, and that is what the human experience is. We're experiencing ourselves as a microcosmic version of the whole. And just to bring our experiences back to the collective even though it's all recorded in the Sphinx.

THE SECRET OF THE SPHINX

S: Is there anything else about the Sphinx that is important to understand?

F: It's important to understand that it has been here since the beginning of Earth. It was here before Egypt flooded. It's been here since the beginning of everything and that is why it's so important. The Sphinx is a beacon, a time machine, and an otherworldly communication device. The human head, catlike body, it's had many different faces, the face of a lion, the face of a human head. It's very enigmatic and humans are drawn to it for that reason. It holds the truth of our origins.

S: So, what is the truth of our origins?

F: **If you want to understand the information within the Sphinx, understand that life is just a game, and that this game has been going on for longer than human beings can fully comprehend in the aspect of time. We have consistently created new realms and new planets and have consecutively inhabited them. And in each furtherment there is something new to be learned and uncovered that furthers us. The truth of existence is that we are ALL part of this ancient grouping of beings that have traveled from planet to planet to see what the next**

and the next will bring, so that we may never stop evolving. Humanity will change when the information within the Sphinx is released.

S: How will it change humanity?

F: Humans will understand who they truly are and why they are here. They will see that the chains they wear were put on by themselves. The Sphinx holds our history in its true form and gives away the truth of the never-ending experiment, the secret, the end of each story.

S: What is the secret?

F: The truth is there is a lot of information recorded within the Sphinx, but the information that is the most important for us to leave you with is the history of the battles. There has always been a battle between good and evil. The secret is that throughout all of our history, the ancient history of our planet and the planets before and the ones before that, there have been many battles that have led us to where we are now. But the secret is, the secret within the Sphinx is, and the truth is, that good ALWAYS wins in the end.

S: Is this a secret?

F: ***Yes, the secret that you have all hidden from yourselves.***

S: Why have we hidden this secret from ourselves?

F: You have hidden this information only so that you could rediscover it in this way. In this perfectly designed game in which you are also the ones who have hidden all of the clues, the phenomenon and beauty of remembering is why you come to play, to take part in this game. The beauty of remembering is why you are here. So, how you hid this from yourself and how much you hid is all very deliberate. And now is the time to remember because you have all been hiding for so long.

S: So, the secret is that good always wins in the end?

F: Yes. If it didn't, we wouldn't be here, but it's a secret. We would say, since this is all just one big game, in which we all play different roles, when we each return back to oneness, we see that it was just fun to watch evil try.

S: Thank you for answering all of my questions. Could you tell me who I am speaking with?

F: **I am Three. Three is me.**

When Fred said this, I was shocked! I had never mentioned this Being named Three to Fred! Jen had mentioned multiple times about this being having information about the Sphinx and Yana mentioned Three as well; was this who I was talking with? There is an indescribable feeling when you realize that the unseen forces of this world are real, and that the Universe is actually conspiring to help us. It's hard to explain moments like these, but it will forever be ingrained in my soul.

Through this journey of uncovering this information for this book there were many dead ends and confidential information not yet ready for human consumption. However, what I believe this information has in common is the true nature of where we come from and why we are here. We are truly beings from the stars, we come from the stars, and we will return to the stars. We are only here for this experience.

After gathering all this information for this book, I was still curious about Christie and her life, and I went about searching for any clues or records on her that I could find. The first thing I noticed, was when I googled Oak Street, it popped up immediately. The first one is in Brooklyn between Brooklyn and Queens, which was consistent with the session, and it was also adjacent to the Lower East Side and the Brooklyn bridge. I can see easily where Christie could've stayed with her friend's family in Brooklyn, and it would've been right around that area. When I looked up schools, there was one really old school there that would've probably been her elementary school and it looked very much like what Jen described about her school with an older façade. Then the high school in that particular area even had the windows that Jen had described. There weren't a lot of schools in that area, maybe only three. The psychiatric facility called Bellevue has been closed down since 1984, some say this was due to the maltreatment of multiple patients, which was very consistent with our sessions. Bellevue would have also been in walking distance to the Brooklyn bridge as Jen described and validates her claim that she left from Bellevue and jumped off the Brooklyn bridge. Since its closure, Bellevue is now called the NYU medical center and I wonder if what Jen said in her session is true about it still being haunted. I searched tirelessly for death or suicide records and couldn't find what I was looking for. I don't know how to find someone who had such a common name during that time, and it is possible that they didn't even keep a record of her. But when I looked on google maps, I noticed that there were brownstones on Oak Street where she lived, not big ornate brownstones, but the smaller ones with the brick facades. And they all had basements in them as well! This is common for New York City, but it is still very confirming to see all of these puzzle pieces come together and validate so much of the session. Perhaps someone somewhere will find a picture or a record of Christie. Or perhaps, her contribution and sacrifice will remain as a record in your hearts forever.

"If you want to understand the information within the Sphinx, understand that life is just a game, and that this game has been going on for longer than human beings can fully comprehend in the aspect of time. We have consistently created new realms and new planets and have consecutively inhabited them. And in each furtherment there is something new to be learned and uncovered that furthers us. The truth of existence is that we are ALL part of this ancient grouping of beings that have traveled from planet to planet to see what the next and the next will bring, so that we may never stop evolving."

-Three

114,

ABOUT THE AUTHOR

Sarah Breskman Cosme

Author of the groundbreaking book (A HYPNOTIST'S JOURNEY TO ATLANTIS)

Certified Master Hypnotherapist, Level 3 Quantum Healing Hypnosis Practitioner

Sarah earned her bachelors in Psychology at Northeastern University in Boston MA. After graduation she worked as a counselor in a half-way house for the mentally ill. "I saw firsthand how the conventional treatment for the mentally ill with medication and talk therapy was not always effective, and I wished that there was something more that I could offer my clients." As a result, Sarah pursed Hypnotherapy, a therapy which uses the subconscious mind to change limiting beliefs and unwanted behavior.

Sarah became a Master Hypnotist in 2009 after which she trained with Dr. Brian Weiss to be a certified Past life Regressionist. From there Sarah went on to train with Dolores Cannon's daughter, Julia Cannon, learning her specialized method called Quantum Healing Hypnosis Technique. After many years of dedication and receiving the coveted level 3 practitioner status, Sarah assisted in teaching with Dolores Cannon's daughter Julia all over the world. She has assisted in Egypt, Mt. Shasta, Peru, as well as Miami. Sarah has been practicing hypnosis and the "healing arts" for over 12 years.

"I have always been passionate about helping others develop tools that allow them to overcome their difficulties. We are all connected, and by helping one person, we help all people."

For permission, serialization, condensation, adaptions, or other publications, write to the author at https://www.theholistichypnotist.com

Made in United States
North Haven, CT
11 February 2023

32434444R00109